The LGBT Rights Movement

Pat Rarus

ReferencePoint
Press®

San Diego, CA

About the Author

Pat Rarus has been a writer-editor of nonfiction literary works
for more than twenty years. She lives in San Diego County.

For more information, contact:
ReferencePoint Press, Inc.
PO Box 27779
San Diego, CA 92198
www.ReferencePointPress.com

LIBRARY OF CONGRESS CATALOGING-IN-PUBLICATION DATA

Name: Rarus, Pat, author.
Title: The LGBT Rights Movement/by Pat Rarus.
Description: San Diego, CA: ReferencePoint Press, Inc., [2019] | Series: The
    Push for Social Change | Includes bibliographical references and index.
Identifiers: LCCN 2018006110 (print) | LCCN 2018007139 (ebook) | ISBN
    9781682824221 (eBook) | ISBN 9781682824214 (hardback)
Subjects: LCSH: Gay rights—United States—Juvenile literature. | Sexual
    minorities—Civil rights—United States—Juvenile literature.
Classification: LCC HQ76.8.U5 (ebook) | LCC HQ76.8.U5 R368 2019 (print) | DDC
    323.3/2640973—dc23
LC record available at https://lccn.loc.gov/2018006110

CONTENTS

IMPORTANT EVENTS IN THE LGBT RIGHTS MOVEMENT

1956
At the meeting of the American Psychological Association, Evelyn Hooker presents research comparing the mental health of homosexual and heterosexual men. Her results show that even skilled researchers find no difference.

1969
The Stonewall riots, named after the gay-friendly bar the Stonewall Inn, take place in New York City's Greenwich Village. Gays protest the raids on the bar, and the event becomes a pivotal, defining moment in the LGBT (lesbian, gay, bisexual, and transgender) rights movement.

1950
Activist Harry Hay founds the Mattachine Society, one of the earliest homophile/homosexual organizations in the United States.

1978
San Francisco supervisor Harvey Milk, an openly gay politician, and Mayor George Moscone are assassinated. To honor both men, city officials hoist the rainbow flag, which becomes a symbol of gay and lesbian pride.

1950   1960   1970   1980   1990

1970
The first gay pride marches are held in multiple cities in the United States on the first anniversary of the Stonewall riots.

1981
The *New York Times* reports that a rare pneumonia and skin cancer is spreading through the gay community. When it is recognized that the virus is found in other populations as well, it is named the acquired immunodeficiency syndrome (AIDS).

1988
US surgeon general C. Everett Koop orders that the brochure *Understanding AIDS* be mailed to every American household.

1953
President Dwight D. Eisenhower signs Executive Order 10450, ordering the dismissal of government workers who engage in so-called sexual perversion. Although the order does not mention homosexuality, hundreds of gays and lesbians lose their jobs as a result.

1973
The American Psychiatric Association removes homosexuality from the *Diagnostic and Statistical Manual of Mental Disorders*, concluding that it is not a mental illness.

4

1993
The US Department of Defense issues the so-called Don't Ask, Don't Tell policy. Under this policy, applicants to the US armed forces would not be asked about nor required to disclose their sexual orientation.

2016
US secretary of defense Ash Carter announces that the Pentagon is lifting the ban on transgender people serving openly in the US military.

2015
On June 26 the US Supreme Court rules (in a 5–4 vote) that states cannot ban same-sex marriage.

1996
President Bill Clinton signs the Defense of Marriage Act, banning federal recognition of same-sex marriage and defining marriage as "a legal union between one man and one woman as husband and wife."

2004
The first legal same-sex marriage in the United States takes place in Massachusetts.

| 1995 | 2000 | 2005 | 2010 | 2015 |

2008
Voters approve Proposition 8 in California, which makes same-sex marriage illegal.

2017
Virginia voters elect the state's first openly transgender candidate to the Virginia House of Delegates. Danica Roem unseats incumbent delegate Bob Marshall, who had been elected thirteen times over twenty-six years.

2010
A federal judge rules that Proposition 8 is unconstitutional.

2012
Tammy Baldwin becomes the first openly gay politician to be elected to the US Senate. She is also Wisconsin's first female senator.

1997
Ellen DeGeneres's character Ellen Morgan, on her self-titled television series *Ellen*, becomes the first leading character to come out as gay on a prime time network television show.

2013
In *United States v. Windsor*, the US Supreme Court strikes down section 3 of the Defense of Marriage Act, ruling that legally married same-sex couples are entitled to federal benefits.

Progress as the Fight Continues

When James Guay was growing up during the 1970s, the evangelical Christian wondered if he would go to heaven even though he was gay. Now a West Hollywood marriage and family therapist specializing in LGBT (lesbian, gay, bisexual, and transgender) issues, Guay recalls the challenges of his youth:

> I was raised in a strict, fundamentalist Christian household in Los Angeles, where homosexuality was referred to as "an abomination to God, worthy of eternal damnation in hell." At church, at school and at home, being gay was rarely acknowledged and, when it was mentioned, described with contempt as the worst sin—comparable to murder, rape and child molestation. I was 9 years old when I recognized my attractions for the same gender. Praying to God every night and pleading with Him to take my feelings away didn't work. Practically living, eating and breathing the Bible didn't work. I tried repressing and denying who I was—but nothing changed inside of me. I was taught by my pastors, parents and peers to hate myself— and that worked.[1]

At age sixteen Guay was pressured to undergo gay conversion therapy, a now-discredited therapy that was intended to transform a person from gay to straight. Guay attended weekly meetings with a Christian psychologist who described himself as an "ex-gay" and underwent various exercises aimed at helping him become more "masculine" and building same-sex nonsexual friendships. The therapy also included dating girls. None of this worked. By age twenty Guay had left home, fallen in love with a man, and eventually built a happy life. As a practicing therapist, he now helps his clients accept and embrace their LGBT orientation. He has also been a vocal opponent of conversion therapy, as he explains: "In fall 2012, California became the first state to ban licensed mental health practitioners from using this practice on minors; I testified in favor of the legislation. I wept when I heard

the news that the bill had been signed into law. And I celebrated when the U.S. Supreme Court recently denied an appeal by anti-gay groups that sought to overturn the ban."[2]

Advances Made but Challenges Remain

As Guay's emotional words show, LGBT rights have advanced a lot since his childhood. Gays can now openly serve in the military and legally marry in all fifty states. Gay characters are now routinely seen on television shows and in the movies. Many gays, like Apple's Tim Cook, serve as executives of Fortune 500 companies and are open about their sexual orientation. Still, challenges remain. After more than twenty years, the Employment Non-Discrimination Act (ENDA)—first introduced to Congress in 1994—has yet to pass. ENDA would make it illegal to fire someone at work because of sexual orientation or gender identity, the same way a person cannot be fired from a job because of race or sex. More recently, Congress introduced another proposed bill, the Equality Act of 2015. If passed, this legislation would provide even more protection than ENDA. It would shield LGBT people from firings at work, evictions from rentals, or refusals of service

LGBT rights have advanced significantly in recent years. Gays can now legally serve in the military and legally marry in all fifty states.

at restaurants or retailers because of their sexual orientation. As of mid-2018, this proposed bill had not yet become law.

Discrimination against members of the LGBT community still exists in other areas besides the workplace. One of these other areas is health care, where gays have sometimes had to wait long hours in hospitals or clinics to receive vital medical treatment or have been refused medical care altogether. In an article about a 2017 national survey, researchers Shabab Ahmed Mirza and Caitlin Rooney write:

Discrimination in health care settings endangers LGBTQ people's lives through delays or denials of medically necessary care. For example, after one patient with HIV disclosed to a hospital that he had sex with other men, the hospital staff refused to provide his HIV medication. In another case, a transgender teenager who was admitted to a hospital for self-inflicted injuries was repeatedly mis-gendered. The word mis-gendered refers to someone, especially a transgender person, using a word, especially a pronoun or form of address that does not correctly reflect the gender with which they identify. The teen, who was discharged early by hospital staff, later committed suicide. Discrimination affects LGBT parents as well: In Michigan, an infant was turned away from a pediatrician's office because she had same-sex parents.[3]

Although much has changed, the LGBT rights movement has more work to do. Some of the biggest challenges ahead involve transgender individuals. According to the Williams Institute, a public policy research center at the University of California, Los Angeles, there are nearly seven hundred thousand transgender people living in the United States. The word *transgender* refers to a person whose gender identity differs from the sex the person had or was identified as having at birth. Despite society's increasingly strong support for gays and lesbians, the American public seems to have a tougher time accepting transgender people, as *Newsweek* reporter Christianna Silver writes: "There is a hard battle ahead for transgender activists. A new study out of the Pew Research Center shows that about a third of Americans still believe society has 'gone too far' in accepting transgender people, even though 40 percent of the country knows someone who identifies as transgender."[4]

> "There is a hard battle ahead for transgender activists."[4]
>
> —*Newsweek* reporter
> Christianna Silver

Even with challenges ahead for transgender individuals, LGBT rights continue to gain momentum. In fact, dramatic progress has been made since the movement first began in 1969.

CHAPTER ONE

The Origins of the LGBT Rights Movement

At 1:20 a.m. on Saturday, June 28, 1969, plainclothes New York City police officers, armed with a search warrant, raided a gay bar and dance club in Greenwich Village called the Stonewall Inn. The Stonewall's managers and bartenders were arrested for selling liquor without a license. For law enforcement at that time, the practice of raiding gay bars was fairly routine. Police would order gay and lesbian patrons to line up, and then they would check their identification. Patrons who were dressed as women were accompanied by female police officers to the restrooms, where they were required to verify their sex. Any men found to be dressed as women would be arrested because cross-dressing was illegal.

But on this night, things did not go as usual. Male patrons wearing women's clothes refused to go with the officers to the restrooms. Also, some of the men who lined up refused to produce their identification. Those who were not arrested were told that they could go home. Police pushed—and even kicked— some of the patrons on their way out of the bar. But rather than go home, many lingered outside. Meanwhile, a group of onlookers had gathered outside the bar to see what was happening. Some called friends, urging them to join the growing crowd. Within minutes, about 150 people had gathered outside. Some of those exiting the bar put on a show for the onlookers. They mocked the cops by bowing, saluting, and hamming it up. The crowd's enthusiasm spurred them on. Author Edmund White, who had been passing by, later recalled his impressions at the time, "Everyone's restless, angry, and high-spirited. No one has a slogan, no one even has an attitude, but something's brewing."[5]

A rumor spread through the crowd that customers who were still inside the bar were being beaten. That really upset the onlookers. When the police wagon arrived to cart away those who had been arrested, some in the crowd threw beer bottles at the vehicle. A brawl broke out when a lesbian in handcuffs was escorted from the door of the bar to the waiting police wagon. The woman broke free of her police escorts a couple of times; she fought with them (punctuated by a lot of swearing and shouting) for about ten minutes. After an officer finally picked her up and hoisted her into the back of the wagon, the woman shouted at onlookers to do something. It was at that point that the crowd went crazy.

Violence Escalates

The police tried to restrain the crowd and knocked a few people down, which incited the crowd even more. The commotion drew even more onlookers. Someone in the crowd shouted that the bar had been raided because the owners did not pay off the cops. Another person yelled that now would be a good time to pay them off. Then coins were flung at the police as the crowd taunted them. Some people also threw beer cans and beer bottles. As police tried to break up the crowd, sometimes forcefully, someone started throwing bricks. By now the crowd had swelled to between five hundred and six hundred people. Outnumbered, the ten police officers barricaded themselves inside the bar along with several of the people who had been arrested and handcuffed. When the protesters became even more unruly by pushing, shoving, and insulting the police, the cops inside the bar drew their guns. The bar doors flew open and officers pointed their weapons at the crowd, threatening to shoot. Someone squirted lighter fluid into the bar and lit a match. The Stonewall Inn started to burn. The fire department and a riot squad were eventually able to douse the flames, rescue those inside, and disperse the crowd. The whole incident had lasted only about forty-five minutes.

In 2015 people drink and socialize at the Stonewall Inn, a now-famous gay bar in New York City. In 1969 riots broke out at the bar as customers and onlookers resisted what was perceived as police harassment of gays.

Michael Fader, one of the club's regular patrons, who was present that night, later recalled,

> We all had a collective feeling like we'd had enough of this. . . . Everyone in the crowd felt that we were never going to go back. It was like the last straw. It was time to reclaim something that had always been taken from us. . . . All kinds of people, all different reasons, but mostly it was total outrage, anger, sorrow, everything combined. . . . There was something in the air, freedom a long time overdue, and we're going to fight for it. It took different forms, but the bottom line was, we weren't going to go away. And we didn't.[6]

Calm and quiet finally came at 4 a.m. Many people stuck around throughout the morning, either sitting on stoops outside the damaged bar or across the street in Christopher Park. Almost everything in the Stonewall Inn had been broken. At first, it seemed the riot was over—but there was still more to come.

The next night, the crowd returned—and it was even larger than the night before. For two hours, protesters demonstrated in the street outside the Stonewall Inn until the police sent a riot-control squad to break them up. The following Wednesday, about one thousand protesters returned to the Stonewall Inn. More demonstrators and police were injured yet again. This time five people were arrested, and looters scavenged local shops.

The entire uproar lasted a total of six days. By the time the riots had ended, a game-changing gay rights movement had been born. Although there had been other protests by gay groups in the past, the Stonewall incident was likely the first time that lesbians and gays saw the value in uniting behind a common cause. The Stonewall riots stimulated the LGBT community to act boldly and continue their activism.

This activism included support from straight people as well as gays. Advocates from nearby Greenwich Village and even people who had not witnessed the riots were inspired to attend organizational meetings to fight for LGBT rights. As transgender activist Sylvia Rivera observed soon after the riots, "Stonewall was the foundation of the modern-day [gay] liberation movement. . . . The riots were an important step on the path from stigma to public awareness and consciousness."[7]

> "Stonewall was the foundation of the modern-day [gay] liberation movement. . . . The riots were an important step on the path from stigma to public awareness and consciousness."[7]
>
> —Transgender activist Sylvia Rivera

A Troubling Label and Even More Troubling Treatments

More than a decade before police physically targeted gays at Stonewall, a respected group of professionals had targeted them in another way. In 1952 the American Psychiatric Association labeled homosexuality a sociopathic personality disturbance that required extensive counseling, diagnostic examinations, and conversion therapy. As in later years, the conversion therapy of this period was designed to change a person's sexual orientation from homosexual or bisexual to heterosexual. But unlike the counseling type of conversion therapy that James Guay underwent during the 1970s, the 1950s version used electric shock and nausea-inducing drugs while the gay or bisexual patient looked at same-sex erotic images. During these sessions, a shock was delivered directly to the patient's genitals (only males were subjected to these treatments) every time he experienced any form of positive response to the same-sex images. Then, opposite-sex erotic images were shown to the patient, with the goal of strengthening heterosexual feelings.

The conversion therapists hoped that the combination of opposite-sex erotic images coupled with shocks to the genitals during the viewing of same-sex images would change a gay person's sexual orientation. Some mental health professionals at the time even claimed a 58 percent cure rate using conversion therapy, but other psychiatric experts disputed this claim, noting that it was not supported by documented evidence or studies.

Gays could also be involuntarily committed to psychiatric facilities by their families. These facilities often promised that patients would be cured of their sexual illness, as it was called, by the time they were ready to leave. Aside from being forced to stay there, patients were often subjected to cruel and inhumane treatments, including conversion therapy, castrations, and lobotomies. Lobotomies, which were once used to treat mental illness, are a surgical procedure in which nerve pathways in one area of the brain are severed from those in other areas. The surgeon most often credited with the rise of lobotomies is Walter Freeman. Freeman is best known for developing a procedure known as a transorbital lobotomy (sometimes called an ice pick lobotomy). In this procedure, the surgeon entered the brain's prefrontal lobe through the patient's eye sockets, using an instrument that resembled a common household ice pick. Of the thousands of lobotomies that Dr. Freeman performed, up to 40 percent of them were on gay patients. Many of these patients, who had been in perfect health

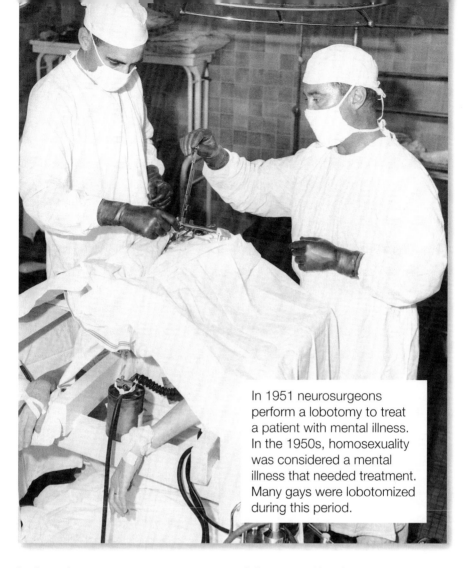

In 1951 neurosurgeons perform a lobotomy to treat a patient with mental illness. In the 1950s, homosexuality was considered a mental illness that needed treatment. Many gays were lobotomized during this period.

before the surgery, were sent to public mental institutions as charity cases until they eventually died. They were completely devoid of emotion. In addition, they could not hold jobs or, in many cases, even carry on conversations. Perhaps saddest of all, many of the lobotomized gay victims were not even acknowledged by their families. As author David Mixner recalls, "The difficulty in documenting so much of this history is that most of the records, history and data have been destroyed. Families were often adamant about not leaving any trace of the overwhelming shame of having a homosexual in the family, and they often erased the gay relative's presence on earth by failing to document."[8]

Widespread Job Discrimination

Because gay individuals were thought to be mentally ill, and mental illness was considered incompatible with holding down a job or advancing a career, gay workers had to hide their homosexuality. They did this in a number of different ways. Some pretended they were romantically interested in the opposite sex by making up stories about a boyfriend or girlfriend. Others escorted female or male friends, relatives, and neighbors to events strictly on a platonic basis but made it seem that these were romantic relationships. Still other gays enrolled in night-school classes, claiming they were studying on weekends and were too busy to date.

Despite these often-elaborate cover-ups, thousands of gays lost their jobs anyway in 1953 when President Dwight D. Eisenhower issued Executive Order 10450. This order banned from federal employment anyone engaged in what it described as sexual perversion. Statistics show that several thousand gays and lesbians lost government jobs. Some were fired. Others resigned rather than face interrogation and the possibility of public disclosure about their personal lives.

It was not until 1973 that a federal judge ruled that a person's sexual orientation could not be the sole reason for termination from federal employment. Two years later, in 1975, the US Civil Service Commission announced that it would consider job applications by gays and lesbians on a case-by-case basis.

The McCarthy Era

Gay workers had other reasons for hiding details about their personal lives from coworkers and others. The 1940s and 1950s marked a period in which Americans feared the growth of communism in Russia, Eastern Europe, and China. During the 1950s, a relatively unknown senator from Wisconsin, Joseph McCarthy, stirred up fear in his congressional colleagues as well as the American public with his allegations that Communists had infiltrated the US government. On February 9, 1950, McCarthy delivered a

An Early Gay Activist Fights the Feds

Gay activist Frank Kameny fought in World War II, earned a doctorate, and then moved to Washington, DC, to work as an astronomer for the Army Map Service. When Kameny was fired from his job in 1957 for being gay, he appealed his firing through the judicial system, losing twice before appealing to the US Supreme Court. In 1961 he argued before the high court that the federal government's treatment of him was an "affront to human dignity." His petition was denied, but this well-publicized refusal garnered public attention for LGBT rights. Four years before the 1969 Stonewall riot, Kameny and other colleagues picketed the White House to protest the arbitrary firing of federal employees because of their sexual orientation. Their goal was achieved eventually. In 1975 the US Civil Service Commission changed its policies so gays were no longer automatically excluded from government employment.

Kameny devoted the rest of his life to gay rights activism. In 2009 he received a formal apology from the federal government for the "shameful action" of being fired for being gay. He was then given the Teddy Roosevelt Award, the highest service honor granted to federal employees.

Although Kameny suffered from heart disease during his last years, he still kept a full schedule of public appearances. He gave his final speech to an LGBT group in Washington, DC, on September 30, 2011. He died less than two weeks later at age eighty-six.

Quoted in Kameny Papers, "APNewsBreak: Gay Rights Papers Shown at US Library," May 8, 2011. www.kameny papers.org.

speech to the Women's Republican Club in Wheeling, West Virginia. During that speech, he proclaimed that he was aware of 205 card-carrying members of the Communist Party who worked for the US Department of State. And then, eleven days later—on February 20—McCarthy turned his attention to gays. In a speech to the Senate, he mentioned two men (although not by name) who he claimed were both Communists and homosexuals. He argued that they and others like them represented a threat to national security. Homosexuals, he said, had "peculiar mental twists."[9]

In McCarthy's view, these peculiarities, coupled with the fear of being found out, made homosexuals even more dangerous than other Communists. He argued that they were susceptible to blackmail by foreign enemy agents. Homosexual men and women with Communist sympathies would divulge government secrets, McCarthy contended, in order to keep their sexual orientation from being exposed.

Organizations Promote Solidarity

An organization was founded in 1950 in Los Angeles to counteract McCarthy's allegations about the homosexual threat to national security. That organization, called the Mattachine Society, was founded by a Communist Party organizer named Harry Hay, but it was not a Communist organization. Rather, its purpose was to promote a sense of solidarity and group identity among homosexuals.

According to Hay, the name *Mattachine* was derived from a medieval French society of unmarried townsmen who performed wearing masks. Their performances were always thinly disguised protests against the aristocracy. Hay said he chose the name because homosexuals in the 1950s were also a masked people, unknown and anonymous, who needed to become engaged in morale building and helping themselves. The Mattachine Society existed as a single national organization headquartered first in Los Angeles and then, beginning around 1956, in San Francisco. Outside of Los Angeles and San Francisco, chapters were established in New York; Washington, DC; Chicago; and other locales. To spread the word about gay rights and bring in new members, the society published a magazine, *One*, which eventually sold about two thousand copies a month.

The Daughters of Bilitis was the counterpart lesbian organization to the Mattachine Society. This was the first lesbian organization in the United States. Although it began as a social club, the organization soon became involved in politics, with the printing of its own magazine, *The Ladder*, which launched in October 1956. The organization's unconventional name was taken from a collection of French poetry, *Les Chansons de Bilitis (Songs of Bilitis)*, which had a lesbian theme. The name also served as a cover-up of sorts. If people became suspicious about the group's activities, they could claim they were a poetry club.

At its peak in 1960, the Daughters of Bilitis had 110 members and five chapters located in San Francisco, New York, Chicago, Providence, and Los Angeles. The group dissolved during the late 1970s because some members favored a stronger feminist stance than that that the Daughters of Bilitis generally advocated. Still, the organization is remembered for providing the first opportunities for lesbians to meet and share their everyday struggles.

Gay-Friendly Bars

Not all gays and lesbians wanted to join organized groups such as the Mattachine Society or the Daughters of Bilitis. Those who did not join, however, had few options for socializing with others in comfort and safety. The challenges of being gay in the United

In 2017 people drink at a LGBT-friendly bar in New York City. Gay bars in major cities across the country acted as safe havens for LGBT people.

Gays Are Normal

Not all mental health professionals thought homosexuals were mentally ill. In 1956 American psychologist Evelyn Hooker conducted an experiment that compared the mental health of homosexual men to heterosexual men. She studied thirty homosexual males and thirty heterosexual males recruited through community organizations. The two groups were matched for age, IQ, and level of education. No one was in therapy at the time of the study. Dr. Hooker administered three different tests that measured patterns of thoughts, attitudes, and emotions. On the basis of her findings, Dr. Hooker asserted that homosexuals were as psychologically normal as heterosexuals. Her work was the first to officially test the assumption that gay men were mentally unhealthy and maladjusted.

In conjunction with other such testing, Dr. Hooker's work led the American Psychiatric Association to remove homosexuality from its *Diagnostic and Statistical Manual of Mental Disorders*. This was a comprehensive classification of officially recognized psychiatric disorders to make sure that mental health professionals agreed on their diagnoses. In 1975 the American Psychological Association (APA) publicly supported this move, stating that homosexuality implies no impairment in judgment, reliability, or general social and vocational capabilities. The APA encouraged mental health professionals to take the lead in removing the stigma of mental illness long associated with homosexual orientation.

States during the 1950s and on into the 1960s sent many LGBT Americans searching for places where they could be themselves, without fear of retribution. Many found safe havens in gay bars and clubs. Dan Savage, an author and gay activist, recalls how it felt when he started going to gay bars:

> I had been told that being gay meant being alone, that being homosexual meant being miserable, that being queer meant being loveless, friendless, and joyless. Then, I walked into a gay bar where I saw men with their friends and men with their lovers. I saw men dancing and I saw men laughing. I found a community that I had been told didn't exist. I found love, I lost love, and I found love again.[10]

Gay bars could be found in New York City, Los Angeles, San Francisco, Oakland, New Orleans, and Seattle. New York City had more gay bars than other cities. Its most famous was the Stonewall Inn, where the LGBT rights movement began in earnest. In fact, many liken the Stonewall riots to the Boston Tea Party because both rebellions led to massive changes. Although several people were injured and the Stonewall building was destroyed, this melee became a defining incident for the LGBT rights movement: the fight was on for equal rights in every part of life.

"I had been told that being gay meant being alone, that being homosexual meant being miserable, that being queer meant being loveless, friendless, and joyless."[10]

—Gay rights activist Dan Savage

CHAPTER TWO

The Movement Organizes

The gay rights movement shifted into high gear soon after the Stonewall riots. Later that summer a group of peace activists and breakaway Mattachines formed the Gay Liberation Front (GLF). Some early members cited anger as the reason the group came together so quickly. Others, like gay activist Jim Fouratt, believed that optimism and determination, not anger, fueled the movement after Stonewall. He recalled, "It was like fire. . . . People were ready. . . . We wanted them to join *us* in making a gay revolution."[11]

Pride

One of the GLF's first actions was to host a series of so-called coming out dances to gain publicity for the organization. Throughout most of 1970, dances were held on college campuses nationwide, encouraging students to be open and proud of their sexuality. As people came out as gay, many of them wanted to actively participate in the movement. The GLF's activism brought new ideas and endeavors. One of these was the first gay pride march in New York City. The organizers formed the Christopher Street Liberation Day Committee, and fittingly, the first LGBT pride parade took place on June 28, 1970, on the first anniversary of the Stonewall riots. The event covered the fifty-one blocks from Christopher Street—the site of the Stonewall riots—to Central Park.

At least two major newspapers covered that first pride march, describing the large number of participants and their passionate fight for LGBT rights. The *New York Times* reported on the front page that the marchers took up the entire street for about fifteen city blocks. The *Village Voice* described the parade as "the out-front resistance that grew out of the police raid on the Stonewall Inn one year ago."[12]

Brenda Howard is known as "the Mother of Pride" for her work in organizing that first march. She also originated the idea for a weeklong series of events around Pride Day, which became the foundation of the annual LGBT pride celebrations that are now held around the world every year. In addition,

> "It was like fire. . . . People were ready. . . . We wanted them to join *us* in making a gay revolution."[11]
>
> —Gay activist Jim Fouratt

Howard, along with LGBT activists Robert A. Martin and L. Craig Schoonmaker, is credited with popularizing the word *pride* to describe these festivities. As LGBT rights activist Tom Limoncelli put it, "The next time someone asks you why LGBT Pride marches exist or why LGBT Pride Month is in June, tell them 'A bisexual woman named Brenda Howard thought it should be.'"[13]

Although the GLF helped organize the first pride march in New York City, not everyone in the LGBT rights movement approved of the organization. Critics said it was a disorganized group without focus. Because the GLF strayed from specific LGBT concerns, the organization lasted less than a year. It did serve a useful purpose, though, in mobilizing the gay rights community into activism.

In its place, a new organization was created. The Gay Activist Alliance (GAA) formed in December 1969. This group had a more specific goal than the GLF: it focused its efforts on issues and actions that would raise the profile of the LGBT community. Through demonstrations and agitation, for example, the GAA forced a prominent New York bar to remove a huge ax labeled *Fairy Swatter* from the wall above the bar. *Fairy* was a commonly used derogatory term for gays. Several GAA activists stormed into the upscale bar and loudly demanded that the ax be taken down immediately. Although they carried no weapons, their forceful words and menacing manner intimidated the straight bar patrons. The GAA activists looked and acted so threatening that

In 1977 members of the Gay Activist Alliance hold a demonstration in New York City. The association focused its efforts on raising the profile of the LGBT community.

the head bartender had no choice but to take down the ax immediately. This was a major victory for the GAA because the bar's management had vowed that there was no way that the ax would ever come down. After that, the bar's frightened customers never returned and the establishment went broke. This sent a message to businesses that homophobic acts (those that show hatred toward LGBT people) do not pay. The GAA was most active from 1970 to 1974.

Zaps Promote the Movement

One of the first strategies used by the GAA to raise public awareness of homophobia was the action they dubbed *the zap*. GAA members would show up at press conferences, society gatherings, television tapings, or anywhere there was a large crowd or an open microphone. Without warning, they would disrupt the event by putting LGBT concerns front and center. New York mayor John Lindsay, who had assured gay rights groups that he would meet with them but never followed up, was the zappers' first target. On April 13, 1970, Lindsay was speaking on the steps of the Metropolitan Museum of Art for its one-hundredth anniversary. All of a sudden, gay activist and GAA cofounder Marty Robinson walked up to Lindsay, leaned into his microphone, and asked, "When are you going to speak out on homosexual rights, Mr. Mayor?"[14] Security guards dragged Robinson away, but soon others were shouting the same question from the crowd.

Lindsay became a prime zap target of GAA activists. Finally, after enduring many such interruptions, he asked Eleanor Holmes Norton, the chairperson of the New York City Commission on Human Rights, to speak with GAA members about employment discrimination. That first conversation with Norton began a relationship that has lasted for decades. Long after the GAA had dissolved, Norton (now in her fourteenth term as congresswoman for the District of Columbia) has continued to champion LGBT rights, including those involving employment.

Making Political Inroads

Lindsay's action marked the beginning of politicians finally paying attention to gay rights during the 1970s. Laws defending gays at work were passed by several cities and states, including East Lansing, Michigan, home to Michigan State University and a hotbed of student activism. In 1972 East Lansing became the first city in the United States to pass a law protecting gays and lesbians from being fired from their jobs solely because of sexual orientation.

The ordinance had been promoted by the Gay Liberation Movement (GLM), a student organization at the university. After the city council voted 4–1 in favor of the law, the GLM's founder, Don Gaudard, reminded the press, "Not everything happens in San Francisco."[15] This remark showed that the LGBT rights movement was making progress in the nation's heartland—the typically conservative Midwest—in addition to the progressive city of San Francisco.

Another midwestern college city, Ann Arbor, home to the University of Michigan, made headlines when citizens elected Kathy Kozachenko of the Human Rights Party to the city council in April 1974. Kozachenko had publicly come out as a lesbian before the election—one of the first politicians to do so in the United States. She served one two-year term before leaving politics. That same year voters in Massachusetts elected Elaine Noble as a state senator. In November 1974 Noble was elected to the state House of Representatives with 59 percent of the vote. Like Kozachenko, Noble had also come out publicly before the race. She served for two terms before deciding not to run for reelection.

The Legendary Harvey Milk

Although Kozachenko and Noble were the first two openly gay individuals elected to public office, Harvey Milk, a small business owner turned politician, garnered the most attention during the 1970s. In late 1972 Milk opened a small camera shop on Castro Street in the center of San Francisco's budding gay community. Milk's sense of humor and great personality won him many friends. About a year later Milk declared his candidacy for the San Francisco Board of Supervisors. He lost the race, but the campaign gave him a chance to develop his political skills.

After some local business owners tried to keep two gay men from opening a store, Milk and a few other merchants started the Castro Village Association. This was an organization of mostly LGBT-owned businesses. Milk was elected president. He then organized the Castro Street Fair in 1974 to attract more customers to area businesses. This became quite a success, inspiring other LGBT communities throughout the United States. After his local business achievements, Milk felt confident to campaign once again for political office. He felt he could make a positive difference not only for the LGBT community but also for other underrepresented groups. During his 1977 campaign for the San Francisco Board of Supervisors, he earned the support of the teamsters, firefighters, and construction unions. His Castro camera store became the center of political activity in the neighborhood. Milk would often pull people off the street to work on his campaign—and most did so with great enthusiasm.

Zapping a Television News Icon

No celebrity escaped zapping, not even the highly respected CBS television news anchor Walter Cronkite. On December 11, 1973, gay activist Mark Allan Segal entered the CBS news studio and jumped between Cronkite and the camera with a handwritten sign that read, "Gays Protest CBS Prejudice." Segal then sat down on Cronkite's desk as 60 million viewers watched the live broadcast. The screen suddenly went blank as studio technicians and producers tackled Segal, tied him up with video cables, and removed him from the studio. The broadcast came back on about three minutes later, with Cronkite calmly reporting, "The young man was identified as a member of something called Gay Raiders, an organization protesting alleged defamation of homosexuals on entertainment programs."

Segal was charged with second-degree criminal trespassing. The trial took place a few months later, with Cronkite called as a witness. During a pause in the trial, Cronkite asked Segal why he zapped him. Segal replied, "Your news program censors. If I can prove it, would you do something to change it?" Segal gave Cronkite examples of biased stories about gay rights and then asked the veteran newsman, "Why haven't you reported on the 23 cities that have passed gay rights' bills?"

Cronkite promised Segal that he would think about his comments. Segal was judged guilty and fined $450. From that time on, Cronkite regularly featured gay and lesbian issues on his news shows, and Segal served as CBS's informal adviser on LGBT issues.

Quoted in Jerome Pohlen, *Gay & Lesbian History for Kids: The Century-Long Struggle for LGBT Rights*. Chicago: Chicago Review, 2016, pp.76–78.

Milk's efforts paid off this time. He won a seat on the San Francisco Board of Supervisors and was inaugurated on January 9, 1978. Milk's election was considered a victory for the LGBT community because San Francisco was known as a trendsetting city. If a gay person like Milk could be elected to an important government position in this famous city, maybe many more LGBT candidates would be elected in other parts of the United States. As a supervisor, Milk accomplished a great deal in a short period of time. According to the Harvey Milk Foundation website:

> A commitment to serving a broad constituency, not just LGBT people, helped make Milk an effective and popular supervisor. His ambitious reform agenda included protecting gay rights—he sponsored an important anti-discrimination bill—as well as establishing day care centers for working mothers, the conversion of military facilities in the city to low-cost housing, reform of the tax code to attract industry to deserted warehouses and factories, and other issues.[16]

In 1977 Harvey Milk, left, sits with San Francisco mayor George Moscone. Milk was one of the first openly gay people in California politics and became a champion of LGBT rights.

Despite Milk's many achievements, many people in the state of California—and across the nation, for that matter—still opposed gay rights. Milk did not let this opposition bother him. Instead, he forged ahead, boldly introducing San Francisco's first gay rights ordinance in 1978, which mandated equal employment rights for job seekers.

Victory and Tragedy

After only a few months in office, Milk took on a big challenge: defeating a statewide initiative that mandated the firing of any California teacher who was gay or who supported gay rights. Milk campaigned across California, speaking out against Proposition 6, which was commonly known as the Briggs initiative for its sponsor, state representative John Briggs. The politically conservative Briggs argued for the passage of Proposition 6 by telling prospective voters, "Homosexuals want your children. If they don't recruit children or very young people, they'll all die away. They have no means of replenishing. That's why they want to be teachers."[17]

Dozens of LGBT activists assisted Milk with his campaign against Proposition 6. These gay activists formed coalitions with unions, low-income workers, and others who felt that they were being ignored by California's mainstream politicians. As part of the campaign to defeat Proposition 6, thousands of LGBT people came out of the closet (revealed that they were gay) and directly confronted the homophobic arguments of those in favor of the proposed law. These grassroots efforts paid off when the Briggs Initiative lost by more than a million votes. The campaign even gained some unexpected allies. Former California governor (and later, US president) Ronald Reagan, a Republican, publicly opposed Prop 6. In an opinion piece for the *Los Angeles Herald-Examiner*, Reagan wrote, "Whatever else it is, homosexuality is not a contagious disease like the measles. Prevailing scientific

> "Whatever else it is, homosexuality is not a contagious disease like the measles. Prevailing scientific opinion is that an individual's sexuality is determined at a very early age and that a child's teachers do not really influence this."[18]
>
> —Former California governor (and later, US president) Ronald Reagan

opinion is that an individual's sexuality is determined at a very early age and that a child's teachers do not really influence this."[18]

Harvey Milk's delight over the defeat of Proposition 6 was short-lived. Milk and San Francisco mayor George Moscone were both shot and killed by former San Francisco supervisor Dan White in November 1978. Shortly after the two murders, White turned himself in to a local police station, accompanied by his wife. As author Jerome Pohlen writes, "Some of the final words on Milk's murder were made by Harvey himself. He knew he could be the target of a crazed homophobe, so he left a tape recording with his will. 'If a bullet should enter my brain, let that bullet destroy every closet door.'"[19]

White faced charges of first-degree murder under circumstances that could have brought the death penalty. However, his defense attorneys painted a picture of him as a lawful person who had served as a firefighter and police officer before running for county supervisor. After ten days of testimony and six days of deliberation, on May 21, 1979, the all-white, all-straight jury convicted Dan White of two counts of voluntary manslaughter. He was sentenced to five to seven years in prison.

> "If a bullet should enter my brain, let that bullet destroy every closet door."[19]
>
> —Harvey Milk, gay rights leader

The jury's verdict caused a quick, violent reaction in what became known as the White Night Riots. About eighteen hundred marchers assembled in the mainly gay Castro area within minutes of the verdict. By the time they reached City Hall 2 miles (3 km) away, the crowd had doubled in size. The protesters stormed City Hall. Some windows in the building were smashed by police to help city officials flee. Other windows were broken by angry demonstrators. Police later fired tear gas in an attempt to disperse the crowd, which had grown to an estimated five thousand. In all, 59 officers and 124 protesters were injured, with about two dozen arrests made. A few weeks later, a civil grand jury convened to find out who ordered the protest, but its investigation ended inconclusively.

The National March on Washington for Lesbian and Gay Rights

A few days before he was murdered, Milk suggested that the LGBT community plan a national march. His inspiration for this event was the 1963 March on Washington for Jobs and Freedom, the largest civil rights gathering of its time and the occasion of the

The Save Our Children Setback

Even while the LGBT rights movement was advancing during the 1970s, setbacks occurred. In 1977 in Florida's Miami-Dade County, lawmakers had passed an ordinance that banned discrimination based on sexual orientation in the areas of housing, employment, and public accommodations such as restaurants, hotels, and stores. Opposition to this new law prompted a bitter political fight between gay activists and conservative Christian fundamentalists. The latter were represented by Anita Bryant—a singer, former beauty queen, and born-again Christian—and the organization she founded, Save Our Children.

Bryant claimed that the ordinance discriminated against her right to teach her children Bible-based morality. She launched a campaign to repeal the ordinance. Within six weeks she gathered enough signatures to put the issue on the ballot.

When the repeal went to a vote, it attracted the largest response of any special election in the county's history, passing by 70 percent. In response to this vote, a group of gay and lesbian community members formed Pride South Florida, now known as Pride Fort Lauderdale. The group's mission was to fight for the rights of the gay and lesbian community in South Florida. Save Our Children was a temporary setback for the gay community in Florida, but the state's LGBT activists would go on to win numerous other victories, including the passage of various antidiscrimination ordinances.

now-famous "I Have a Dream" speech by Martin Luther King Jr. Milk's goal was to direct political attention to LGBT concerns just as that march had done for the civil rights movement. Nearly a year after his death—on October 14, 1979—some two hundred thousand gay men, lesbians, bisexuals, transgender people, and straight allies attended the first National March on Washington for Lesbian and Gay Rights. The demonstration served to nationalize the gay rights movement, which before had been focused on local struggles and local victories.

As the enthusiastic crowd chanted, "We are everywhere!" the march began at the National Mall and ended in a rally near the Washington Monument. The march was led by the Salsa Soul Sisters, the oldest black lesbian organization in the United States. Washington, DC, mayor Marion Barry welcomed the marchers on behalf of the city. But it was the marchers themselves who exuded a new sense of purpose. "For us the feeling of being there and marching in the nation's capital was amazing—the sense of community, of solidarity," recalls Penelope Tzougros, now a finan-

In 1987 over fifty thousand people participate in the second National March on Washington for Lesbian and Gay Rights. The march was inspired by the first National March on Washington for Lesbian and Gay Rights, which occured in 1979 and had served to nationalize the Gay Rights Movement.

cial planner in Waltham, Massachusetts. "The whole experience was phenomenal because for the first time in our lives it felt like we were in the majority."[20]

In addition to the march itself, the organizers arranged three days of workshops featuring artistic events, strategy sessions, focus groups on specific issues of women and minorities within the LGBT community, consciousness raising, local organizing, religion, and other issues. The Monday after the march was organized as the Constituent Lobbying Day. On this day, five hundred people attempted to contact every member of Congress to express support for gay rights legislation. The participants met with 50 senators and more than 150 House members.

The 1970s had been a rewarding decade for the LGBT movement. The notion that homosexuality was a mental illness had been discredited and abandoned. Gay politicians were elected to public office and fought for LGBT rights. Pride events were launched in cities across the country (and eventually around the world). The National March on Washington demanded attention and action for LGBT equality by federal officials. But the decade to come would test the LGBT community's resolve perhaps more than ever before.

CHAPTER THREE

How AIDS Mobilized the Movement

Life was improving for gays and lesbians in America at the start of the 1980s. Awareness of LGBT issues was growing, antidiscrimination laws were gaining support and being enacted, and people felt freer than they had in the past to be themselves. But the good feelings were about to come to an abrupt end. The year 1981 marked the start of a series of events that would baffle many of the brightest minds in the medical research community and would destroy the lives of millions—starting with the gay community.

Larry Kramer, a successful author and screenwriter, was vacationing on Fire Island, a small barrier island off the coast of New York's Long Island, in the summer of 1981. While there, Kramer happened to notice a *New York Times* story headlined, "Rare Cancer Seen in 41 Homosexuals."[21] The story ran on page twenty, which made it easy for readers to miss it. Still, many in the gay community (including Kramer) read the story and were shaken. Kramer was surprised to learn that eight of the victims died within two years of receiving a diagnosis. As the *Times* reporter, Lawrence K. Altman, wrote,

> The cause of the outbreak is unknown, and there is as yet no evidence of contagion. But the doctors who have made the diagnoses, mostly in New York City and the San Francisco Bay area, are alerting other physicians who treat large numbers of homosexual men to the problem in an effort to help identify more cases and to reduce the delay in offering chemotherapy treatment.[22]

After thinking more about the story, Kramer made a disturbing personal connection: some of his gay friends in their twenties and thirties had died recently without much warning. Could they have gotten this strange new sickness?

A Terrifying New Sickness

Sprinting into action, Kramer contacted Alvin Friedman-Kien, the investigating physician of New York University Medical Center, whose name had appeared in the *Times* story. Kramer also contacted Lawrence Mass, a gay physician friend. Kramer then decided to hold a meeting with influential gay men to see what could be done to combat this new illness.

Eighty gay men met with Dr. Friedman-Kien in Kramer's apartment on August 11, 1981. The physician explained that for reasons still unknown, previously healthy gay men were dying from an unusual type of skin cancer known as Kaposi's sarcoma as well as from a certain type of pneumonia. Laboratory tests indicated that the patients' immune systems, which would typically protect people from these diseases, were greatly run-down. At that time, no one knew why. Kramer's August meeting raised nearly $7,000 and launched the Gay Men's Health Crisis (GMHC) organization, which was the first organized response to fighting this puzzling disease.

One of the first acts of the GMHC was to set up a crisis counseling hotline in the home of one of its members. Through this hotline, people could share information about what was, at the time, being called gay-related immunodeficiency disease (GRID). Eventually, medical researchers came to understand that gay men were not the only ones affected; the disease, which was renamed acquired immunodeficiency syndrome (AIDS), was killing both men and women, both gay and straight.

New York City was more affected by the AIDS epidemic of the 1980s than any other American city. Still, the West Coast had its share of AIDS victims as well. For that reason, a nonprofit organization in California followed the lead of the GMHC. In April 1982 a group of community leaders and physicians joined forces to create the San Francisco AIDS Foundation. They first operated out of a small office on Castro Street with a dedicated team of volunteers providing basic medical information, resources, and referral services. By the fall of 1982 the foundation's single-telephone hotline had become nationally recognized for providing accurate AIDS information. As a result, San Francisco quickly became a central resource point for other groups forming across the nation.

In October 1982, as fears grew, members of the San Francisco AIDS Foundation traveled south to Los Angeles. They gave a presentation to four friends who were interested in starting a similar group. Building on the experience in San Francisco, the Los Angeles group set up their own hotline—on a single telephone staffed by volunteers in a storage room at the Los Angeles Gay and Lesbian Community Services Center. Through the hotline they gathered

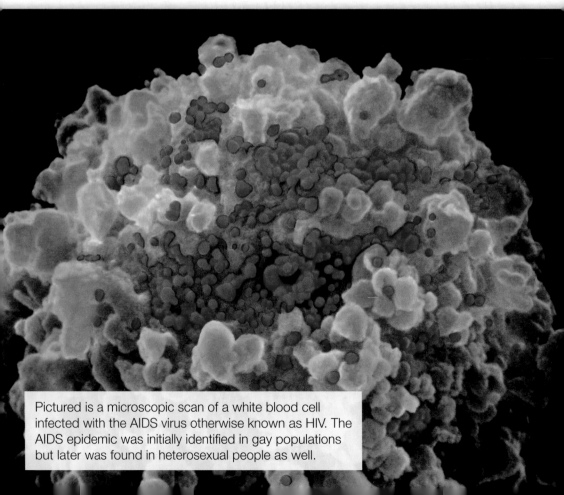

Pictured is a microscopic scan of a white blood cell infected with the AIDS virus otherwise known as HIV. The AIDS epidemic was initially identified in gay populations but later was found in heterosexual people as well.

whatever information they could find and answered people's questions as best they could. Most of the information available at the time fit on a single page. Realizing that funds were needed to educate the community and prevent the spread of the disease, the founders of the Los Angeles group enlisted the help of other friends and held a benefit party. They raised more than $7,000, which became the seed money for a new organization. Recognizing that AIDS was not just a gay disease (researchers were also discovering high numbers of infected individuals among intravenous drug users), the founders named their new group AIDS Project Los Angeles.

Fund-Raising as a Matter of Life and Death

After it became obvious that a nationwide health crisis was developing, in late 1982 the federal government stepped up by authorizing $5.6 million for AIDS research. That money was a start—but just a start. In San Francisco, Los Angeles, Phoenix, Chicago, Atlanta, New York City, and Washington, DC—metropolitan areas with large gay populations—AIDS activists found ways to boost funding for AIDS research and community support. They organized dances, concerts, talent contests, comedy shows, and other activities. Celebrities from New York City's theatrical world lent their time and talents to AIDS-related fund-raisers. These celebrity performers were both gay and straight. The idea was that if famous people supported AIDS research, then others less well-known and less wealthy would also support the cause, and they did. During the early 1980s, most US residents had little knowledge of AIDS. The general public still thought of it as mainly a problem for gays and drug users—not something other people had to worry about. This made the work of gay activists all the more important, according to author David Román, who writes:

> Throughout 1982 and 1983, critical years in the history of AIDS, in cities across the United States, performance became the primary way for AIDS service organizations

to raise money for research and direct services, distribute information and educate local constituencies and recruit volunteers to strengthen a grassroots community response to AIDS. Underfunded by government and state institutions, if funded at all, these grassroots organizations depended upon these [fund-raising] benefits.[23]

> "Throughout 1982 and 1983 . . . performance became the primary way for AIDS service organizations to raise money for research and direct services, distribute information and educate local constituencies and recruit volunteers to strengthen a grassroots community response to AIDS."[23]
>
> —David Román in his book *Performance, Gay Culture & AIDS*

Without a doubt, the highest-profile and most profitable early AIDS fund-raising event was the Ringling Bros. and Barnum & Bailey Circus held at New York's Madison Square Garden on April 30, 1983. The sold-out event—with more than seventeen thousand people, mostly men, attending—netted $250,000 for the GMHC. In addition to providing much-needed funds for AIDS research, the circus event increased awareness of the devastating disease and demonstrated yet again the importance of working together for a cause that meant so much to so many people. Román writes:

Demonstrating support for gays at the circus event that day were two famous performers: Conductor Leonard Bernstein and opera star Shirley Verrett. Bernstein gallantly strode across the center stage in his white dinner jacket and conducted "The Star-Spangled Banner" while opera star Shirley Verrett sang this patriotic song with pride. Gay men and their friends in the audience cheered wildly. Gay activist Larry Kramer later said that this was "one of the most moving events I have ever experienced."[24]

Unprotected Sex Is the Culprit

Definitive answers about AIDS finally began emerging in 1983. Researchers began to learn that the virus that causes AIDS—the human immunodeficiency virus, or HIV—is spread primarily through sexual contact regardless of whether the participants are gay or straight. Blood transfusions and shared needles were also to blame. The US Public Health Service issued its first recommendations for preventing the transmission of HIV through sexual contact and blood transfusions in January 1983. Armed with that knowledge, community organizations across the country began distributing condoms. It was an important time in the early fight against HIV/AIDS. Also in 1983, the San Francisco AIDS Foundation distributed free condoms in that city. It was one of the first major outreach efforts to stop the spread of this epidemic.

In June 1983 a coalition of foundation staff members and supporters marched in San Francisco's gay pride parade. As they made their way down Market Street, they handed out thousands of condoms to spectators. Not only were they putting a lifesaving

In 2012 a member of the AIDS Healthcare Foundation distributes condoms to promote safe sex. The US Public Health Service began promoting the use of condoms in 1983 once it determined that HIV was transmitted sexually.

tool into people's hands, they were also educating both gay and straight individuals about how HIV is transmitted. They showed how all people could protect themselves.

Firing Up the LGBT Rights Movement

Ironically, the onset of the AIDS epidemic probably fired up the LGBT movement more than any other single event in its history. It united people who, up to this point, had thought of themselves as having very different priorities. In particular, gay men and lesbians felt they had little in common other than their same-sex identities. As lesbian scholar Lillian Faderman observes, this changed with the AIDS crisis:

> Many lesbian feminists felt that men were chauvinistic and unsympathetic to women in general, and gay men were no different from straight men. Lesbian separatists particularly cut themselves off [and] wanted to have nothing whatsoever to do with any kind of male, gay or straight. But things changed seriously in the 1980s with the AIDS epidemic. . . . Lesbians realized that with the disaster of AIDS, this was no time for animosity. . . . Gay men realized that these are our sisters and we need to work with them.[25]

"Things changed seriously in the 1980s with the AIDS epidemic. . . . Lesbians realized that with the disaster of AIDS, this was no time for animosity. . . . Gay men realized that these are our sisters and we need to work with them."[25]

—Lesbian scholar Lillian Faderman

With so many gay men being lost to AIDS, lesbians became actively involved in helping those who were suffering and dying. They opened food banks and worked in hospitals. It became especially important for women with nursing or other types of medical backgrounds to persuade their colleagues in the medical establishment to give the best-possible treatment to AIDS-infected patients. Lesbians had to run interference for those ill

Mama's Kitchen

In 1990 Laurie Leonard, a volunteer at a San Diego food bank offering free food to AIDS patients, learned that some of the afflicted clients were too weak to come in for meals. Leonard, whose brother had died of AIDS, persuaded volunteers to prepare and deliver free home-cooked meals to San Diegans suffering from AIDS. Soon afterward, she founded the nonprofit Mama's Kitchen.

At first, fund-raising was a challenge because many people did not want to deal with AIDS. The organization got a real boost when marketing executive Jonathan Bailey volunteered as a fill-in driver and then joined the board of directors in 1995. Bailey, who had relocated from San Francisco to San Diego for work, knew from living in the Bay Area with its AIDS activism how vital such activism and community outreach were. Largely due to Bailey's efforts and influential contacts, the fund-raising tide began turning during the late 1990s, with high-profile charity events and wealthy supporters who contributed to them.

Since it began in 1990, Mama's Kitchen has prepared and delivered over 8 million meals. In 2017, 79 percent of its home-delivered hot meal service went to people infected with HIV.

with AIDs because many straight doctors and nurses were terrified of the mysterious new disease. They avoided AIDS patients—sometimes even refusing to enter their hospital rooms.

When straight nurses refused to work in AIDS medical wards, lesbian nurses took their places. Because they had experience fighting for their own medical issues, lesbians ensured that infected gay men received prompt medical care. They pushed wheelchairs, visited the ill, and emptied the patients' bed pans.

A Famous Actor Comes Out

In 1985 the US government licensed a blood test to detect the AIDS virus. Also, the American Association of Blood Banks and the American Red Cross began screening the national blood supply to prevent infected blood from being given to ill patients needing transfusions. Still, overall efforts to find drugs to treat, and perhaps cure, AIDS were moving slowly.

The AIDS crisis still did not resonate with most mainstream Americans—that is, until A-list actor Rock Hudson revealed that he had the disease. Hudson had become famous during the 1950s and 1960s for playing romantic leading men, so it was a shock to many that he was both gay and HIV positive. Hudson came out in the summer of 1985 and died in October of that year. Only two weeks earlier, President Ronald Reagan, a former actor and friend of Hudson's, spoke the word *AIDS* in public. It was the first time the US president had done so, and it raised the disease's public profile one more notch. By then, nearly six thousand people in the United States had already died from the disease, and thousands more were dying in countries around the world.

The Surgeon General Steps Up

It took until October 1986 for the federal government to take the AIDS crisis seriously. Surgeon general C. Everett Koop issued a critical thirty-six-page report that requested substantially more money for AIDS research and public education than had initially been allocated. In a 1986 editorial, the *New York Times* quoted Koop's reason for requesting more funding:

> Many people, especially our youth, are not receiving information that is vital to their future health and well-being because of our reticence in dealing with the subject of sex, sexual practices, and homosexuality. This silence must end. We can no longer afford to sidestep frank, open discussions about sexual practices—homosexual and heterosexual. Education about AIDS should start at an early age so that children can grow up knowing the behaviors to avoid to protect themselves from exposure to the AIDS virus.[26]

In addition to his government report, Koop wrote an explicit eight-page brochure titled *Understanding AIDS*. In 1988 he ordered it to be mailed to every American household—107 million in all. Congress approved and paid for the mailing, which cost $17 million.

Koop's brochure—written in easy-to-understand language—discussed the dangers of anal sex, urged the use of condoms, and contained advice on how to talk to children about AIDS. The brochure contained small photographs, including those of two women with AIDS, and appealed to the public to show compassion and support for those who were infected. Koop, an evangelical Christian, defied expectations from both the political left and right through his bold approach to addressing AIDS, especially his call for frank talk and comprehensive sex education.

> "Education about AIDS should start at an early age so that children can grow up knowing the behaviors to avoid to protect themselves from exposure to the AIDS virus."[26]
>
> —Surgeon general C. Everett Koop

ACT UP

Whereas Koop was frank and outspoken about preventing AIDS, activist and author Larry Kramer was obsessive about it. He cut ties with the GMHC during the early 1980s because he felt the group was too passive. He urged the GMHC to hold politicians accountable for the lack of available medication instead of just helping victims who were already sick. Most of all, Kramer blamed the US Food and Drug Administration (FDA) because he claimed that this government agency was taking too long to approve new experimental drugs and treatments. In a New York City speech at the Lesbian and Gay Community Service Center on March 10, 1987, Kramer called for immediate action: "Every one of us here is capable of doing something. Or doing something strong. We have to go after the FDA—fast. This means coordinated protests, pickets, and arrests. Are you ashamed of being arrested?"[27]

Two days after that speech, Kramer helped establish the AIDS Coalition to Unleash Power (ACT UP) in New York City. The group's goal was to demand the release of experimental AIDS drugs. Its members were a diverse, nonpartisan group, united in anger and committed to direct action to end the AIDS crisis. That first chapter began with about three hundred members. Other chapters soon formed in various parts of the country.

Nine days after ACT UP was formed, the FDA made an important announcement regarding the status of a possible new drug for treating AIDS. The agency said it had sufficient documented drug-testing results to allow the use of azidothymidine (AZT), a drug developed by the British pharmaceutical firm Burroughs Wellcome. The drug was fast-tracked for approval, and in a record time of twenty months, it became available for AIDS treatment on March 19, 1987.

In 1991 ACT UP members march in protest. The AIDS Coalition to Unleash Power (ACT UP) began in 1987 with a commitment to directing resources to end the AIDS epidemic.

A Straight Scientist Educates and Organizes

Iris Long, a retired research chemist who was heterosexual, heard one of Larry Kramer's speeches in New York City soon after he formed ACT UP in 1987. She was impressed with Kramer's passion but felt his lack of knowledge would sink his efforts to get the government and pharmaceutical industry to speed up development of affordable and effective AIDS treatments. Kramer later recalled that Long challenged him to shape up his approach. "You guys don't know diddly about what this is. Anybody who wants to learn how the science works, how everything works, how the NIH [National Institutes of Health] works, how the FDA works, how you can deal with this enormous amount of material, I'll teach you."

Long delivered on everything she promised. She had a unique ability to explain complex drugs and drug trials to the group's members. Through her efforts, they came to understand which drugs were most promising and why. They also learned the language and concepts that enabled them to converse with the people and entities doing the work.

Long's other important contribution was the founding of the AIDS Treatment Data Network. This network enrolled AIDS patients in clinical drug trials at hospitals around the country. When interviewed years later about her activism, Long remarked, "I was always a laboratory person. . . . I was not a joiner before, at all. But, I was a fighter type person that would fight for somebody's rights."

Quoted in Jerome Pohlen, *Gay & Lesbian History for Kids: The Century-Long Struggle for LGBT Rights.* Chicago: Chicago Review, 2016, pp. 109–10.

Iris Long, interview by Sarah Schulman, "Iris Long Interview," ACT UP Oral History Project, May 16, 2003. www .actuporalhistory.org.

The AIDS Crisis Strengthens the Movement

The onset of AIDS was horrific in so many ways. Thousands of previously healthy gay men and soon others were dying from a disease that doctors and medical researchers initially did not understand and could not prevent or successfully treat. In the absence of factual information, fear and hostility were growing. Employees were fired from their jobs because of rumors that they had AIDS or knew people who did. Despite the havoc that AIDS unleashed during the 1980s, it produced one positive outcome: the life-threatening illness united and strengthened the LGBT rights movement as never before.

CHAPTER FOUR

The Movement Goes Mainstream

During the AIDS crisis of the 1980s, many closeted gays came out to their families, coworkers, and employers. Even if they were not sick themselves, they wanted to help others who were ill, or at least show their support for the LGBT rights movement. As gays became more open about themselves, no longer feeling the need to hide, society in general also began accepting the idea of homosexuality. This new openness became evident even in Florida, which had been a 1970s battleground in the fight for LGBT rights. In 1990, for example, LGBT activists persuaded Palm Beach County officials to pass laws protecting county workers from discrimination on the basis of sexual orientation. LGBT activists in Florida also felt the time was right for their own kind of gay pride celebration—one more for pleasure rather than protest—and they had the perfect venue in mind.

Gay Day at the Magic Kingdom

In 1991, in the central Florida city of Orlando, the activists decided to hold an event at Disney World, one of the area's most popular tourist attractions. Called Gay Day, the event's purpose was to celebrate the progress made by the LGBT rights movement. Although the Walt Disney Company was not a sponsor of Gay Day, its management agreed to host the event. LGBT organizers chose the first Saturday in June as the first Gay Day to commemorate the Stonewall uprising, which had also occurred in June. Holding this gathering at the Disney theme park resonated with the LGBT community, as *Time* reporter John Cloud writes: "The event sparked something in the gay imagination. For many gays and lesbians who grew up in the latter half of the 20th century, childhood was a time of anxiety and secrets, faggot jokes and spitballs. There was, literally and figuratively, no *Glee*. Going on the teacup ride or getting wet on Splash Mountain was a way to reclaim an unfinished adolescence."[28]

> "Going on the teacup ride or getting wet on Splash Mountain was a way to reclaim an unfinished adolescence."[28]
>
> —*Time* magazine reporter John Cloud

Gay Day at Disney World became a popular annual event—attracting about ten thousand gays and lesbians from all parts of the country in 1995 alone. In 1997 Disney further extended its hospitality by renting out Typhoon Lagoon to Gay Day for an after-hours party, a practice that continues today. By

In 1991 LGBT activists organized a Gay Day event at the popular Disney World theme park in Orlando, Florida. Disney management did not sponsor the event but agreed to host it.

1998 Orlando flew rainbow flags—symbols of the LGBT rights movement—downtown to welcome visitors to Gay Day. This was also the year that Disneyland in Anaheim, California—the original site of the Magic Kingdom—hosted its own Gay Day celebration, which continues today.

Domestic Partner Benefits Gain Support

By welcoming LGBT visitors to the first Gay Day in 1991, Disney demonstrated a willingness to enact gay-friendly policies and practices. In 1995 the entertainment company began offering

Apple CEO Tim Cook Talks About Being Gay

Tim Cook is the chief executive officer (CEO) of Apple. In 2014 he became the first executive of a Fortune 500 company to publicly identify as gay. Cook knows he serves as a role model for many, including LGBT persons who may be struggling with their sexuality. In an online *Bloomberg Technology* article, he frankly discusses gay pride:

> While I have never denied my sexuality, I haven't publicly acknowledged it either, until now. So, let me be clear: I'm proud to be gay, and I consider being gay among the greatest gifts God has given me. Being gay has given me a deeper understanding of what it means to be in the minority and provided a window into the challenges that people in other minority groups deal with every day. It's been tough and uncomfortable at times, but it has given me the confidence to be myself, to follow my own path, and to rise above adversity and bigotry. It's also given me the skin of a rhinoceros, which comes in handy when you're the CEO of Apple.
>
> I don't consider myself an activist, but I realize how much I've benefited from the sacrifice of others. So, if hearing that the CEO of Apple is gay can help someone struggling to come to terms with who he or she is, or bring comfort to anyone who feels alone, or inspire people to insist on their equality, then it's worth the trade-off with my own privacy.

Tim Cook, "Tim Cook Speaks Up," *Bloomberg Technology*, October 30, 2014. www.bloomberg.com.

health care coverage to the partners of gay and lesbian employees. This was an important step. Until this time, only spouses and children were eligible for coverage under employee health insurance plans at most companies. Because same-sex marriage was not legal in any state, these and other standard employee benefits were generally not available to the partners of gay and lesbian workers. Around that same time, other major employers, including Microsoft, Levi-Strauss, Xerox, and Stanford University, also initiated domestic partner benefits. These changes—this growing mainstream support—represented an important shift in attitudes toward the LGBT community. LGBT individuals who had once been forced to hide their true selves were now being viewed by many companies just like any other member of the workforce. And these employers began changing their policies to reflect this view.

This attitude is now prevalent among all sorts of businesses, according to the nonprofit organization Human Rights Campaign Foundation. Each year this organization publishes a comprehensive report, the *Corporate Equality Index (CEI)*, which is considered the national benchmarking tool on corporate policies and practices concerning LGBT employees. As the 2018 edition of the index states, there are now six hundred companies with perfect scores of one hundred. Its authors write,

> From tech startups to construction companies to auto manufacturers, major businesses—employing millions of Americans—are ensuring that their workplaces are fully LGBT inclusive. On a practical level, this means that millions of LGBT workers across America—as well as LGBT workers employed by multinational companies around the globe—are covered under non-discrimination policies and able to bring their full selves to work every day. CEI also continues to see major businesses including transgender employees. In fact, the number of employers offering transgender-inclusive health care coverage increased from 647 in 2016 to 750 in 2017—an impressive 58 percent of Fortune 500-ranked businesses.[29]

Still Waiting for Federal Laws

Even before major US employers voluntarily offered domestic partner benefits to gay employees, the federal government was grappling with LGBT rights. The Employment Non-Discrimination Act, commonly known as ENDA, was first introduced in Congress in 1994. This act, if passed, would prohibit discrimination in the workplace on the basis of sexual orientation and gender identity. A variation of this bill has been introduced in some form in every Congress since then but has yet to win full congressional approval. In the meantime, another, similar bill, the Equality Act of 2015, has been introduced. If passed, it would go beyond ENDA to protect LGBT people from being fired, evicted, or denied service because of their sexual orientation. Like ENDA, this bill has also failed to win congressional approval.

In the absence of any federal law, the only workplace protections for LGBT individuals are found in state laws, according to *Fast Company* magazine's Rich Bellis, who writes, "The states that actually bar [workplace] discrimination for both sexual orientation and gender identity in both the public and private sector are still in the minority: 20 do so, plus the District of Columbia."[30]

California is one of those twenty states. The California Fair Employment and Housing Act (FEHA) prohibits discrimination and harassment due to sexual orientation or gender identity in employment. *Gender identity* refers to a person's own self-identification as a man or woman or male or female, regardless of his or her anatomical sex at birth. That said, both types of discrimination, whether due to gender identity or sexual orientation, are illegal under FEHA.

The Military

One major employer, the US military, has a mixed record in dealing with LGBT personnel. It took the military a lot longer than other employers to welcome gays into its workforce, but even the military has joined this group. With more than 3 million workers on its payroll, the military is considered the largest employer in the world. As such, its policies and practices touch a lot of lives. As blogger and retired US Air Force sergeant Rod Powers writes,

> During World War II, the Korean War, and the Vietnam War, the military defined homosexuality as a mental defect and officially barred gays from serving based on medical criteria. However, when more soldiers were needed due to combat, the military developed a habit of relaxing its screening criteria. Many homosexual men and women served honorably during these conflicts. Unfortunately, these periods were short-lived. As soon as the need for soldiers decreased, the military would involuntarily discharge them.
>
> It wasn't until 1982 that the Department of Defense officially put in writing that "homosexuality was incompatible with military service." According to a 1992 report by the Government Accounting Office, nearly 17,000 men and women were discharged under this new directive during the 1980s.[31]

Military policy toward LGBT personnel changed again in 1993, when a new law signed by President Bill Clinton went into effect. Under that law, military recruiters were instructed not to ask, pursue, or harass about sexual orientation when signing up men and women to serve in the US Army, Navy, Marines, Air Force, and Coast Guard. Under the new law, military personnel would not be asked about their sexual orientation and would not be discharged simply for being gay. However, having sexual relations, displaying romantic overtures with members of the same sex, or telling anyone about

> "During World War II, the Korean War, and the Vietnam War, the military defined homosexuality as a mental defect and officially barred gays from serving based on medical criteria."[31]
>
> —Blogger and US Air Force sergeant Rod Powers

their sexual orientation was considered "homosexual conduct"[32] under the policy and was a basis for involuntary discharge.

Clinton hoped that the Don't Ask, Don't Tell (DADT) policy, as it came to be known, would make it possible for gays to serve in the military without fear of being found out and dismissed from service. The effect was not quite what he had intended.

Darren Manzella was a US Army sergeant when he learned firsthand about the real-world effects of the new law. In 2008, while he was still in Iraq, Manzella—who is gay—was contacted by the Service Members Legal Defense Network, a national nonprofit organization offering legal assistance to those affected by the DADT law. The group's representative told Manzella that a television network was looking for a gay serviceman in a combat zone to tell his story. After weighing the risk of being discharged for speaking out publicly, Manzella agreed to do the interview, which aired just a few days before his return to the United States. In June 2008, a few days after his return, Manzella was notified that he was being discharged from the military under the DADT policy. He was given an honorable discharge, which allowed him to keep his military benefits, including health care insurance and a pension. His discharge papers read "homosexual conduct admission."[33]

During the period in which the DADT policy was in force, the military discharged more than thirteen thousand lesbians, gays, and bisexuals, according to the Service Members Legal Defense Network. A 2005 government report found that about eight hundred of these military personnel had skills deemed critical, including in engineering and linguistics. Experts have noted that the cost of losing experienced service members and then recruiting and training replacement personnel amounted to hundreds of millions of dollars.

The Repeal of Don't Ask, Don't Tell

The DADT policy might have benefited some individuals, but in December 2010 Congress repealed the law, deciding it had hurt

Supporters of Repeal "Don't Ask, Don't Tell" (DADT) rally in Washington, DC, in 2010. Congress repealed the law in 2011.

more than it had helped. President Barack Obama signed the repeal legislation on December 22. The policy officially ended the following year on September 20, 2011. The law's repeal began a new chapter for the nation's military.

In the weeks that followed the repeal, a series of first-ever newsworthy events attracted media attention. The Marine Corps was the first branch of the armed services to recruit from the LGBT community. Gay and lesbian service members previously discharged under DADT had the opportunity to reenlist; reservist Jeremy Johnson became the first such person to reenlist.

In other first-ever events after the DADT repeal, the Department of Defense granted permission for military personnel to wear their uniforms while participating in the San Diego Pride Parade in July 2012. Good news also occurred on the legal front after the DADT repeal. On January 7, 2013, the American Civil Liberties Union (ACLU) reached a settlement with the federal government in the case of Richard Collins, a decorated former staff sergeant in the US Air Force who served for nine years until he was discharged from service under the policy. Collins's superiors learned that he was gay when two civilian coworkers observed him exchange a kiss with his civilian boyfriend. Collins received an honorable discharge from the Air Force but discovered after the discharge had been completed that his separation pay had been cut in half on the grounds of homosexuality. The ACLU's lawsuit, entitled *Collins v. United States*, made it possible for Collins and other gays in the military to receive their full separation pay upon discharge under DADT.

Gay and lesbian individuals can now serve in the military without fear of retribution. But there is still one group of LGBT individuals whose situation in the military is less certain. In January 2018 a new law went into effect that allows transgender people to also serve openly in the US military. Before the law's official passage, there already were trans people in the military—by some

Coming Out After Don't Ask, Don't Tell

Army colonel Janet Holliday has served in the military for nearly thirty years. From the time she began her army career in 1992 until 2011, when Don't Ask, Don't Tell (DADT) was repealed, not even Holliday's closest friends knew that she was a lesbian. In an interview with the US Army Press, Holliday recalled that she was involved in a couple of investigations early in her military career that, "pushed me so far back in the closet I was in the next room."

Holliday, who came out at age forty-five after DADT was repealed, said she felt a tremendous amount of freedom to finally be herself. Still, it was difficult for her to tell people she had known for twenty years that she was gay. "I had a few (straight) friends that, I think, were really hurt by the fact that they felt like I couldn't trust them. But they were in the military and I didn't want to put them in a position of knowing something they might have to report. That is why I didn't tell anybody."

In 2012 Holliday met the love of her life: US Air Force colonel Ginger Wallace. Reflecting on the DADT policy, Holliday mused, "Ginger and I have 54 years of active service combined. If we had been separated from [military] service because of orientation, that wouldn't have happened. How many years of service has the military missed out on because of policies like DADT?"

Quoted in Rachael Tolliver, "Commander Recalls LGBT Journey," US Army, May 26, 2016. www.army.mil.

accounts, as many as 15,500. But most were afraid to come out. The new federal law signaled a welcome change. However, in March 2018 President Donald Trump announced plans to ban most transgender people from military service. As of mid-2018, no one could say for sure how this issue would play out. As CNN reporter Sophie Tatum writes,

> The White House said the [revised] policy will say "transgender persons with a history or diagnosis of gender dysphoria—individuals who the policies state may require substantial medical treatment, including medications and surgery—are disqualified from military service except under certain limited circumstances.". . . According to a Pentagon memo about the policy, exceptions to the ban include people who have been "stable for 36 consecutive months in their biological sex prior to accession," service members who "do not require a change of gender" and troops who started serving under the Obama administration's policy prior to the new memo.[34]

Gay Characters in Entertainment

The mainstream status of the LGBT community is more settled in the entertainment industry. In recent decades LGBT performers have had more freedom to be themselves than people in many other segments of American life, but in television and movie portrayals of the 1970s, 1980s, and most of the 1990s, gay characters were often depicted through stereotypes. That began changing as more viewers saw their LGBT relatives and friends coming out. It meant that television and movie characters had to be more believable. After all, LGBT people held down jobs, had partners, and lived a lot like straight people. They could no longer be portrayed as jokes. Now LGBT characters appear often in online videos and mainstream television shows. The long list includes

Modern Family, *Orange Is the New Black*, *Mr. Robot*, *Game of Thrones*, *Transparent*, and many more.

Back in 1997, though, television executives were much more conservative in their programming choices. At that time, the first primetime television show involving a gay main character was called *Ellen*. The star of the series was Ellen DeGeneres, then a closeted lesbian. DeGeneres chose to come out via a *Time* magazine cover story that read, "Yep, I'm Gay."[35] That public ad-

Popular talk show host and actress Ellen Degeneres revealed she was gay in 1997. Initially her acting career suffered but she eventually prevailed with her successful daytime talk show.

mission caused less commotion than the announcement that her on-screen character, bookstore owner Ellen Morgan, would be coming out as well.

Some big-name sponsors, such as Wendy's and the Chrysler Corporation, withdrew their sponsorship of the show, but DeGeneres insisted that her television series air the episode of her character coming out. On April 30, 1997, some 42 million viewers tuned in. As the season continued, the ABC network began each episode with a warning: "Caution: This Show Contains Adult Content." After lower television ratings during the next season, *Ellen* was canceled. DeGeneres claimed that television shows had no problem showing unmarried people having sex or depicting violent programs where people kill each other. So, what was the big deal about showing two women holding hands? "I lost my entire career, and I lost everything for three years," she told *W* magazine in 2007. "I was so angry; I was just so angry. I really worked my way up to a show, a sitcom that was mine that was successful, that was on for five years. I did what was right: I came out, which was good for me, and ultimately it was the only thing I could do. And then I got punished for it."[36]

> "I came out, which was good for me, and ultimately it was the only thing I could do. And then I got punished for it."[36]
>
> —Celebrity Ellen DeGeneres

DeGeneres was proud of what she had done, and in the end, she won big. She went on to be the voice of Dory in two animated movies, *Finding Nemo* and later *Finding Dory*. Her greatest success of all came in 2003, when she launched a popular daytime television talk show that is still airing today. The show had won fifty-nine Daytime Emmy Awards as of 2017, including four for Outstanding Talk Show and six for Outstanding Talk Show Entertainment.

With corporations, the military, and the media recognizing LGBT rights, great progress was made during the 1990s. Still, one major lifestyle right remained elusive: the right to marry. That, too, would soon change.

CHAPTER FIVE

Marriage Equality at Last

Even as gays and lesbians gained more civil rights during the 1990s, they yearned for one of the most personal freedoms of all: the right to marry legally. Over time this right had been granted to gay and lesbian couples in some states but not others. By early June 2015, thirty-seven states and the District of Columbia had recognized gay marriage. In the rest of the states, a gay or lesbian couple could hold a marriage ceremony if they wished, but it was not considered a legal arrangement. This changed on June 26, 2015, when the US Supreme Court ruled (on a 5–4 vote) that states must license same-sex marriages and recognize similar unions from other states. The ruling ended a years-long legal battle over marriage rights for gays and lesbians. Justice Anthony Kennedy authored the ruling that legalized same-sex marriage in all fifty states. In the final paragraph of that ruling, Kennedy wrote,

> No union is more profound than marriage, for it embodies the highest ideals of love, fidelity, devotion, sacrifice, and family. In forming a marital union, two people become something greater than once they were. As some of the petitioners in these cases demonstrate, marriage embodies a love that may endure even past death. It would misunderstand these men and women to say they disrespect the idea of marriage. Their plea is that they do respect it, respect it so deeply that they seek to find its fulfillment for themselves. Their hope is not to be condemned to live in loneliness, excluded from one of civilization's oldest institutions. They ask for equal dignity in the eyes of the law. The Constitution grants them that right.[37]

Celebrations at Stonewall

Earlier that week, the Stonewall Inn—the site of the 1969 riots that ushered in the modern LGBT rights movement—was officially declared a historical landmark. When the Supreme Court's same-sex marriage ruling was announced that Friday, hundreds of people—gay and straight, young and old—gathered at the Stonewall Inn to honor early gay rights leaders and celebrate the Supreme Court decision. Reactions ranged from cries of relief, jumps for joy, and excited applause. For so many of those gathered outside the Stonewall Inn, that Friday brought a breakthrough they had never envisioned as taking place during their lifetimes.

Among those in the crowd were Jeff Mead and Peter Born, a gay couple who had married in California in 2008 during the brief window of time between when the state legalized same-sex marriage and the passage of Proposition 8, a state constitutional amendment that banned it. A *Time* magazine reporter captured their emotions: "When I graduated from high school—Catholic high school—in 1983, I didn't even think that this would ever be on the map," said Mead. Born agreed, and grabbing Mead's hand, he added, "It's a big change. Especially for guys our age, who have come through the AIDS crisis and are still here. We're excited and proud to be gay and be gay Americans and to be married as a gay couple after so many years together."[38]

> "We're excited and proud to be gay and be gay Americans and to be married as a gay couple after so many years together."[38]
>
> —Peter Born, an engineer in San Francisco

California's Setback Before the Supreme Court Ruling

Prior to the Supreme Court ruling, the fight over same-sex marriage had been both nasty and noisy in many states—and California was no exception. Proposition 8 had passed in 2008 with

In 2008 protesters demonstrate against California's Proposition 8. The controversial proposition stated that only marriage between a man and woman would be legally valid in the state.

53 percent of the vote. The constitutional amendment stated that "only marriage between a man and a woman is valid or recognized in California,"[39] reversing a previously protected right.

Led by evangelical Christians and the Catholic and Mormon churches, the "Yes on 8" campaign played on people's emotions. Author Jerome Pohlen describes some of the claims made by Proposition 8 backers:

> One television commercial showed a young girl telling her mother, "Guess what I learned in school today. I learned how a prince married a prince, and I can marry a princess!" The ad went on to say that without Prop 8, same-sex marriage would be part of the school curriculum. Other commercials claimed that all churches would be forced to perform same-sex marriages. Neither was true.[40]

The California ban on same-sex marriages lasted less than two years. In 2010 chief US district judge Vaughn Walker in San

Francisco ruled that Proposition 8 was unconstitutional under the US Constitution and barred its enforcement. "Proposition 8 fails to advance any rational basis in singling out gay men and lesbians for denial of a marriage license. Indeed, the evidence shows Proposition 8 does nothing more than enshrine in the California Constitution the notion that opposite-sex couples are superior to same-sex couples,"[41] said Walker.

The First Same-Sex Marriage on Record

Although California has long been known for taking controversial stands on many issues, the fight for same-sex marriage actually began decades earlier in Minneapolis, Minnesota. Two gay young men, Jack Baker and Michael McConnell, met via a mutual friend in 1966. When Baker asked McConnell for a committed relationship, McConnell said he would agree only if they could be legally married. There had never been a legal same-sex marriage in the United States, but Baker promised to find a way.

In 1969 Baker enrolled in law school at the University of Minnesota. While doing research during his first semester, he learned that the Minnesota marriage statutes did not mention gender. Therefore, he reasoned, there was no basis in the law for not allowing same-sex marriage. Baker and McConnell went to the courthouse to apply for a marriage license on May 18, 1970. Hennepin County clerk Gerald R. Nelson allowed them to apply but refused to grant the license. The resulting publicity cost McConnell his job.

Late in 1970 Baker and McConnell sued the Hennepin County District Court. They argued that since same-sex marriage was not explicitly illegal under Minnesota law, they must be issued a marriage license. In 1971 a county district court judge denied their motion without comment. Baker and McConnell appealed the decision. The case was set to be heard by the Minnesota Supreme Court later that year.

The Adoption Angle

Meanwhile, Baker discovered a way to legalize their union. But instead of being joined in marriage, they would become a family through adoption. Baker had learned that adoption provides most of the legal family benefits of marriage, such as Social Security eligibility, income tax breaks, and veterans' benefits. So, on August 3, 1971, McConnell adopted Baker. On the adoption papers, Baker legally changed his name to Pat Lyn McConnell. He chose a gender-neutral first name so that he and McConnell could try applying for another marriage license in a new county. There was no Minnesota law against marrying someone whom you had adopted. "I could see that once we did the adoption and did the name change, that we could reapply for the marriage license and probably make it happen,"[42] Baker said.

> "I could see that once we did the adoption and did the name change, that we could reapply for the marriage license and probably make it happen."[42]
>
> —Minnesota attorney Jack Baker

And, in fact, that is what happened. The two men were married on September 3, 1971, by Methodist minister Roger Lynn. It was the first legal same-sex marriage in the United States. "It was kind of a whirlwind thing," McConnell said of the ceremony, which took place in a friend's home. "We had about 12 or 13 friends, the minister and our best men. And that was about it."[43]

On October 15, 1971, a little more than a month after the marriage, the Minnesota Supreme Court upheld the Hennepin County clerk's decision not to issue the first marriage license the couple had applied for (the ruling became known as *Baker v. Nelson*). Determined to keep fighting, the couple appealed to the US Supreme Court. On October 10, 1972, the Supreme Court dismissed the case because it did not raise any federal constitutional issues. For that reason, the state's ruling stood.

The Love Story That Helped Legalize Gay Marriage

When the Supreme Court announced its 2015 decision to legalize same-sex marriage, Jim Obergefell, the plaintiff in the landmark case *Obergefell v. Hodges*, felt vindicated yet profoundly sad. John Arthur, his husband and partner of more than twenty years, did not live long enough to experience this milestone.

Obergefell and Arthur had wanted to marry for a long time. In 2013, after the Supreme Court struck down the Defense of Marriage Act, the couple decided the time to take that step had come. They made this decision knowing that their married life would not last long; Arthur was terminally ill and confined to his bed. Their own state of Ohio had banned gay marriage in 2004, so they picked a state where same-sex marriages were legal—Maryland—to tie the knot there. Given Arthur's health, the only way to do this was to hire the services of a costly medical charter jet. Obergefell turned to Facebook. Hearing about their plans, family and friends donated $13,000—enough to cover the cost of transportation. The couple was married on the tarmac at the Baltimore-Washington International Airport. Three months later, Arthur died.

Sometime later, a civil rights attorney reached out and explained that when Arthur died, his death certificate would state that he was unmarried since Ohio did not recognize the marriage. "They were going to say, 'No you don't exist,'" said Obergefell, who was born and raised in the Buckeye state. "It ripped our hearts out. So, we filed suit against Ohio."

Stav Ziv, "How Jim Obergefell's Fight for His Dying Spouse Legalized Gay Marriage in America," *Newsweek*, June 26, 2015. www.newsweek.com.

A Case in Hawaii

The defeat in the Minnesota case did not end efforts to obtain marriage rights for same-sex couples, but two decades passed before the next big court challenge. During the 1980s another gay couple, Ninia Baehr and Genora Dancel, wanted to buy joint health insurance and name each other as beneficiaries on their life insurance policies. But their home state of Hawaii would not allow it because they were not legally married. So the couple tried to obtain a marriage license at the Department of Health's vital records office in Honolulu. They and two other same-sex couples were refused. In May 1991 all three couples filed a discrimination suit against the state. Four months later a judge dismissed their claim. Baehr and Dancel appealed to the Hawaii Supreme Court, which sent the case back to the lower court for retrial. This decision was based on the fact that Hawaii's constitution specifically outlawed discrimination based on sex.

Opponents of same-sex marriage worried about the case in Hawaii. They knew that a ruling allowing same-sex marriage in one state could lead to similar outcomes in other states. They also worried what would happen if a same-sex couple vacationing in Hawaii got married and then tried to force their home state to recognize the marriage. Conservative and evangelical Christians soon joined forces. In addition to holding prayer meetings and other events, they urged their elected officials to outlaw same-sex marriages.

Gay couple, Ninia Baehr and Genora Dancel, were denied a marriage license by the state of Hawaii. In 1991 they joined two other couples in filing a discrimination suit against the state.

In the fall of 1996 Congress began debating the Defense of Marriage Act (DOMA), a proposed bill that would prevent any legally married same-sex couple from receiving any of the many federal benefits given to married couples, such as filing joint tax returns, receiving Social Security survivor benefits if a partner died, spousal inheritance, and others. As author Jerome Pohlen explains, "It also nullified (made invalid) the 'full faith and credit' clause of the U.S. Constitution for same-sex marriage. No state would be required to honor a gay marriage performed in another state."[44]

The DOMA debate was brief but at times heated. Proponents of DOMA argued forcefully that legalizing same-sex marriage would destroy the sacred bond of marriage. Opponents argued equally forcefully that loving couples who choose marriage honor that sacred bond whatever their sexual orientation. Among those in Congress who spoke out against DOMA were Representative Nancy Pelosi of San Francisco. Pelosi talked about a lesbian couple, Del Martin and Phyllis Lyon, who lived in her district: "Their commitment, their love, and their happiness are a source of strength to all who know them. Their relationship is not a threat to *anyone's* marriage."[45] Unlike Pelosi, Representative Steve King of Iowa was an outspoken DOMA supporter. Equal protection, he said in an interview, means "equal protection for a man and woman to be able to get married to each other," because "that's been the definition of marriage for thousands of years."[46] DOMA passed the House by a huge majority of 342 to 67, or 84 percent of the vote. It passed the Senate by an even bigger percentage—85 to 14, or 86 percent of the vote. Many LGBT activists viewed DOMA's passage as an effort by conservatives to embarrass President Clinton just before the 1996 election and to alienate his LGBT supporters. They were right on both counts.

DOMA Becomes Law

Clinton had been an early and strong supporter of LGBT rights. He was the first US president to choose openly gay people for government jobs. So when Clinton signed DOMA in the middle of the night on September 21, 1996, members of the LGBT community were stunned. The prevailing view was that Clinton signed the bill because he feared not signing it would jeopardize his chances for reelection. With the election less than two months away and polls showing a tight race with his Republican opponent, Senator Robert Dole, Clinton decided not to do anything that might hurt his chances with moderate voters.

Years later Richard Socarides—an LGBT advocate, lawyer, writer, and political commentator—presented his view of Clinton's decision to sign DOMA:

> Inside the White House, there was a genuine belief that if the President vetoed the Defense of Marriage Act, his re-election could be in jeopardy. There was a heated debate about whether this was a realistic assessment, but it became clear that the President's chief political advisers were not willing to take any chances. Some in the White House pointed out that DOMA, once enacted, would have no immediate practical effect on anyone—there were no state-sanctioned same-sex marriages then for the federal government to ignore. I remember a Presidential adviser saying that he [Clinton] was not about to risk a second term on a veto, however noble, that wouldn't change a single thing nor make a single person's life better.[47]

Although DOMA was not formally repealed, all of its provisions were struck down as a result of the US Supreme Court's 2015 ruling in *Obergefell v. Hodges*. Same-sex couples now have the right to marry in every state; consequently, every state must recognize lawful same-sex marriages performed in other states.

Stances Taken by the Next Presidents

President Clinton won reelection. When his second term ended, Americans elected Republican George W. Bush as president.

Overcoming Challenges

In August 2014, San Diego–based LGBT couple Nurith Amitai and Kwilanzo Zuree "KZ" Crawford married in a pirate-themed ceremony aboard the *Star of India*, a San Diego landmark and the world's oldest active sailing ship. Amitai, a native of Germany with a doctorate in neuroscience, moved to California in 1997 on a student visa (later followed by a postdoctoral visa). After a job layoff in late 2012, her entire future depended on her pending green card application—if her petition were denied, she could be deported. In 2013 Amitai was granted her green card, securing her legal status.

Crawford is transgender; although assigned female at birth, he identifies as male. He served as a US Marine for eighteen years. After retirement from the military, Crawford transitioned medically and socially to a masculine identity. Amitai is white; Crawford is black. Amitai is Jewish; Crawford was raised Christian and now identifies as spiritual, though not religious. Despite the many challenges, they were able to marry. They are now the proud parents of a two-year-old. When asked about the challenges along the way, Amitai replied, "Yes, it's a different world now, and we've come far. Still, we can't let our guard down—ever."

Nurith Amitai Crawford, interview with the author, October 2017.

Bush also served two terms, from 2001 until 2009. Bush described himself as a "compassionate conservative." For example, despite the Republican Party's opposition to civil unions as an alternative to same-sex marriage, Bush supported the idea of civil unions. During a campaign speech in October 2004, the incumbent president running for reelection said, "I don't think we should deny people rights to a civil union, a legal arrangement, if that's what a state chooses to do so."[48]

Even during his first term, Bush showed some acceptance toward gays and lesbians. He was the first Republican president to appoint an openly gay man to serve in his administration. That appointment went to Scott Evertz, who served as director of the Office of National AIDS Policy. Also during Bush's first term, his nominee Michael E. Guest became the first openly gay man to be confirmed by the Senate as a US ambassador. He became ambassador to Romania in September 2001.

The appointments of Evertz and Guest were well publicized. In addition, though, numerous closeted gays served in the Bush administration. One former senior official, whose office included at least three gay staffers, commented on this when he said, "Did we have a lot of people in the closet in the administration? . . . I used to say we had an entire warehouse."[49]

There was no need for closeted gays when Barack Obama succeeded Bush as president, serving two terms from 2009 until 2017. Less than halfway through his first term, President Obama had already appointed more openly gay officials than any other president in history. One news report noted that estimates from gay activists put the total number of appointments by the middle of 2010 at 150—a number that exceeded the 140 such appointments made by Clinton during his entire two terms in office. "It's both significant and rather ordinary," said Michael Cole, a spokesman for the gay rights group Human Rights Campaign in 2010. "It's a simple affirmation of the American ideal that what matters is how you do your job and not who you are."[50]

Obama took various actions that advanced LGBT rights. In addition to putting a historic number of LGBT people in high-ranking government positions, he helped lift the ban on LGBT people serving openly in the military. He also granted to federal contractors protections against discrimination on the basis of sexual orientation and gender identity. And, although he initially supported civil unions over making gay marriage legal, Obama later announced his support for legalizing gay marriage.

Another High-Profile Case

Despite the progress made for LGBT rights, the movement's work is not done. In June 2018 the US Supreme Court ruled on a Colorado case involving a same-sex couple who wanted to buy a custom-made wedding cake and the baker who refused to sell them one. Colorado has a law against discrimination based on sexual orientation. The baker contended that forcing him to make

David Mullins (left) and Charlie Craig (right) are the gay couple who challenged a Colorado baker's refusal to create a cake for their wedding. The two men were photographed outside the US Supreme Court building on the day the justices heard their case.

a wedding cake for a same-sex couple violated his rights to free speech and the free exercise of religion. The high court ruled that the baker was a victim of religious bias on the part of the state's civil rights commission but also stressed the importance of maintaining equal rights for gays and lesbians. Other similar cases will likely be heard in the future.

LGBT rights supporters can reflect on the achievements of the past as they focus their efforts on the future. Their fight may not be easy, but it will be worth the effort. As Thomas Paine, an eighteenth-century English-born American political activist, author, political theorist, and revolutionary, said in his classic book *The American Crisis*: "What we obtain too cheap, we esteem too lightly: it is dearness only that gives every thing its value. Heaven knows how to put a proper price upon its goods; and it would be strange indeed if so celestial an article as freedom should not be highly rated."[51]

SOURCE NOTES

Introduction: Progress as the Fight Continues

1. James Guay, "My Hellish Youth in Gay Conversion Therapy and How I Got Out," *Time*, July 15, 2014. www.time.com.
2. Guay, "My Hellish Youth in Gay Conversion Therapy and How I Got Out."
3. Shabab Ahmed Mirza and Caitlin Rooney, "Discrimination Prevents LGBTQ People from Accessing Health Care," Center for American Progress, January 18, 2018. www.american progress.org.
4. Quoted in Christianna Silver, "A Third of Americans Say Society Has 'Gone Too Far' in Accepting Transgender People," *Newsweek*, November 8, 2017. www.newsweek.com.

Chapter One: The Origins of the LGBT Rights Movement

5. Quoted in David Carter, *Stonewall: The Riots That Sparked the Gay Revolution*. New York: St. Martin's, 2010, p. 148.
6. Quoted in Carter, *Stonewall*, p. 160.
7. Quoted in Jerome Pohlen, *Gay & Lesbian History for Kids: The Century-Long Struggle for LGBT Rights*. Chicago: Chicago Review, 2016, p. 65.
8. David Mixner, "LGBT History: The Decade of Lobotomies, Castration and Institutions," July 28, 2010. www.davidmixner.com.
9. Quoted in Judith Adkins, "'These People Are Frightened to Death': Congressional Investigations and the Lavender Scare," *Prologue*, Summer 2016, vol. 48, no. 2. www.archives.gov.
10. Dan Savage, "What We Find in Gay Bars and Queer Clubs," *Stranger*, June 15, 2016. www.thestranger.com.

Chapter Two: The Movement Organizes

11. Quoted in Pohlen, *Gay & Lesbian History for Kids*, p. 72.
12. Quoted in Kathleen LaFrank, ed., "National Historic Landmark Nomination: Stonewall" National Park Service, January 1999. www.nps.gov.
13. Tom Limoncelli, "In Memoriam, Brenda Howard," New York Area Bisexual Network, July 27, 2005. www.nyabn.org.

14. Quoted in Pohlen, *Gay & Lesbian History for Kids*, p. 75.
15. Quoted in Pohlen, *Gay & Lesbian History for Kids*, p. 80.
16. Harvey Milk Foundation, "The Official Harvey Milk Biography." http://milkfoundation.org.
17. Quoted in Pohlen, *Gay & Lesbian History for Kids*, p. 86.
18. Quoted in Pohlen, *Gay & Lesbian History for Kids*, pp. 89–90.
19. Quoted in Pohlen, *Gay & Lesbian History for Kids*, p. 93.
20. Quoted in Pohlen, *Gay & Lesbian History for Kids*, p. 95.

Chapter Three: How AIDS Mobilized the Movement

21. Lawrence K. Altman, "Rare Cancer Seen in 41 Homosexuals," *New York Times*, July 3, 1981. www.nytimes.com.
22. Altman, "Rare Cancer Seen in 41 Homosexuals."
23. David Román, *Performance, Gay Culture & AIDS*. Bloomington: Indiana University Press, 1998, p. 20.
24. Román, *Performance, Gay Culture & AIDS*, p. 19.
25. Quoted in Kira Brekke and Brook Sopelsa, "11 Lesbians In History You Don't Know But Should," *Huffington Post*, October 16, 2015. www.huffingtonpost.com.
26. Quoted in "The Surgeon General Dr. Koop Defends His Crusade on AIDS," *New York Times* (editorial), October 26, 1986. www.nytimes.com.
27. Quoted in Pohlen, *Gay & Lesbian History for Kids*, p. 109.

Chapter Four: The Movement Goes Mainstream

28. Quoted in John Cloud, "How Gay Day Made a Home at Disney," *Time*, June 10, 2010. www.time.com.
29. Chad Griffin, "Letter from the HRC Foundation President," in *Corporate Equality Index 2018: Rating Workplaces on Lesbian, Gay, Bisexual, Transgender, and Queer Equality*, by Human Rights Campaign Foundation, January 2018, p. 2. www.hrc.org.
30. Rick Bellis, "Here's Everywhere in the U.S. You Can Still Get Fired for Being Gay or Trans," *Fast Company*, August 28, 2017. www.fastcompany.com.
31. Ron Powers, "Policies Concerning Homosexuals in the U.S. Military: History of the Policies of the Armed Forces for Gay and Lesbian Service Members," The Balance, December 22, 2017. www.thebalance.com.
32. Quoted in Powers, "Policies Concerning Homosexuals in the U.S. Military."
33. Quoted in Pelin Sidki, "Discharged Under 'Don't Ask, Don't Tell,'" CNN, November 10, 2009. www.cnn.com.

34. Quoted in Sophie Tatum, "White House Announces Policy to Ban Most Transgender People from Serving in Military," CNN, March 24, 2018. www.cnn.com.

35. Quoted in Maxwell Strachan, "When Ellen Came Out, She Didn't Just Change Lives. She Saved Them," *Huffington Post*, April 28, 2017. www.huffingtonpost.com.

36. Quoted in Strachan, "When Ellen Came Out, She Didn't Just Change Lives."

Chapter Five: Marriage Equality at Last

37. Quoted in Justia, "Obergefell v. Hodges, 576 U.S. (2015)." https://supreme.justia.com.

38. Quoted in Jacob Koffler, "Crowds at Stonewall Inn Celebrate Gay Rights Victory Decades in the Making," *Time*, June 26, 2015. www.time.com.

39. Quoted in Pohlen, *Gay & Lesbian History for Kids*, p. 144.

40. Pohlen, *Gay & Lesbian History for Kids*, p. 144.

41. Quoted in CNN Wire Staff, "Judge Overturns California's Ban on Same-Sex Marriage," August 5, 2010. www.cnn.com.

42. Quoted in Julie Compton, "Gay Couple Pens Memoir After 45 Years of Marriage," NBC News, October 10, 2016. www.nbcnews.com.

43. Quoted in Compton, "Gay Couple Pens Memoir After 45 Years of Marriage."

44. Pohlen, *Gay & Lesbian History for Kids*, p. 127.

45. Quoted in Pohlen, *Gay & Lesbian History for Kids*, p. 128.

46. Quoted in Nina Totenberg, "DOMA Challenge Tests Federal Definition Of Marriage," National Public Radio, March 26, 2013. www.npr.org

47. Quoted in Richard Socarides, "Why President Clinton Signed the Defense of Marriage Act," *New Yorker*, November 8, 2013. www.newyorker.com.

48. Quoted in Garance Franke Ruta, "George W. Bush's Forgotten Gay-Rights History," *Atlantic*, July 8, 2013. www.theatlantic.com

49. Quoted in Timothy J. Burger, "Inside George W's Closet," *Politico*, July/August 2014. www.politico.com.

50. Quoted in Fox News, "Obama Appoints Record Number of Gay Officials," October 26, 2010. www.foxnews.com.

51. Thomas Paine, *The Writings of Thomas Paine, Vol. 1 (1774–1779),* Collected and Edited by Moncure Daniel Conway. New York: G.P. Putnam's Sons, 1894). http://oll.libertyfund.org/titles/343.

Books

Ann Bausum, *Stonewall: Breaking Out in the Fight for Gay Rights*. New York: Speak, 2015.

Adrian Brooks, *The Right Side of History: 100 Years of LGBTQ Activism*. New York: Cleis, 2015.

Lillian Faderman, *The Gay Revolution: The Story of the Struggle*. New York: Simon & Schuster, 2015.

Cleve Jones, *When We Rise: My Life in the Movement*. New York: Hachette, 2016.

Michael McConnell with Jack Baker, as told to Gail Langer Karwoski, *The Wedding Heard 'Round the World: America's First Gay Marriage*. Minneapolis: University of Minnesota Press, 2016.

Kevin L. Nadal, *That's So Gay! Microaggressions and the Lesbian, Gay, Bisexual, and Transgender Community*. Washington, DC: American Psychological Association, 2013.

Nancy Orel and Christine Fruhauf, *The Lives of LGBT Older Adults: Understanding Challenges and Resilience*. Washington, DC: American Psychological Association, 2014.

Jerome Pohlen, *Gay & Lesbian History for Kids: The Century-Long Struggle for LGBT Rights*. Chicago: Chicago Review, 2016.

Internet Sources

Gabriel Arana, "The Most Urgent Queer Political Battles to Fight in 2018," Them, January 1, 2018. www.them.us/story/the-most-urgent-queer-political-battles-to-fight-in-2018.

John Aravosis, "Yes Virginia, Corporate America Played an Important Role in the LGBT Rights Revolution," *American Blog*, June 11, 2017. http://americablog.com/2017/06/yes-virginia -corporate-america-played-important-role-lgbt-rights-revolution .html.

Molly Ball, "How Gay Marriage Became a Constitutional Right: The Untold Story of the Improbable Campaign That Finally Tipped the U.S. Supreme Court," *Atlantic*, July 15, 2015. www.the atlantic.com/politics/archive/2015/07/gay-marriage-supreme -court-politics-activism/397052.

Kira Brekke, "How Lesbians' Role in the AIDS Crisis Brought Gay Men and Women Together," *Huffington Post*, April 4, 2017. www.huffingtonpost.com/entry/aids-crisis-lesbians_us_5616867 ae4b0e66ad4c6a7c4.

Tim Cook, "Tim Cook Speaks Up," *Bloomberg Technology,* October 30, 2014. www.bloomberg.com/news/articles/2014-10-30 /tim-cook-speaks-up.

Kelsey Dallas, "U.S. Supreme Court Justices Signal Masterpiece Cakeshop Case Will Be Difficult Decision," *Deseret News*, December 5, 2017. www.deseretnews.com/article/900005183/us -supreme-court-justices-signal-masterpiece-cake-case-will-be -difficult-decision.html.

Chris Johnson, "U.S. Agency to Congress: Pass Law Against LGBT Workplace Discrimination," *Washington Blade*, November 29, 2017. www.washingtonblade.com/2017/11/29/u-s-agency -to-congress-enact-law-against-lgbt-workplace-discrimination.

Ron Powers, "Policies Concerning Homosexuals in the U.S. Military: History of the Policies of the Armed Forces for Gay and Lesbian Service Members," The Balance, December 22, 2017. www .thebalance.com/policy-concerning-homosexuals-us-military -3347134.

Websites

American Civil Liberties Union (ACLU) (www.aclu.org). The ACLU is one of the nation's oldest civil rights watchdog groups. Its mission is to defend and preserve the individual rights and liberties guaranteed to every person in America. The ACLU has branches in each state that provide information on issues affecting young people, including how to get involved with the organization.

Gay, Lesbian & Straight Education Network (www.glsen.org). Devoted to change, GLSEN works with students, schools, parents, and the community to ensure that students in the LGBT community are safe in their school environments. The organization offers training and support at the national and local levels for educators, principals, district leaders, and government leaders on how to embrace the differences of LGBT students.

GLAAD (www.glaad.org). Formerly the Gay and Lesbian Alliance Against Defamation, GLAAD advocates for LGBT rights and holds the media accountable for the image it presents to the public about the LGBT community. By increasing awareness, GLAAD hopes to decrease the stigma, stereotyping, and marginalization of those within the LGBT community.

Human Rights Campaign (www.hrc.org). The Human Rights Campaign is the largest LGBT civil rights advocacy organization. HRC operates at both a grassroots level and nationally. Its website offers a trove of information on LGBT legal rights at both the state and national levels. HRC's popular logo, a yellow equal sign with a dark blue background, conveys the organization's mission: to achieve equal rights for LGBT people.

Human Rights Watch (www.hrw.org). Human Rights Watch is a nonprofit organization that conducts research and publishes and disseminates reports on human rights violations across the globe. HRW puts pressure on governments and international organizations to reform abusive practices. The organization provides internships in field offices throughout the world.

International Lesbian, Gay, Bisexual, Trans, and Intersex Association (www.ilga.org). ILGA seeks to promote LGBTI equality through the worldwide cooperation and mutual support of its members. The organization focuses public and government attention on cases of discrimination against LGBTI people by supporting programs and protest actions, applying diplomatic pressure, and working with international organizations and the international media.

National LGBTQ Task Force (www.thetaskforce.org). The National LGBTQ Task Force works to build a future where everyone is free to be themselves in every aspect of their lives. The task force trains and mobilizes millions of activists throughout the nation to remove the barriers that LGBTQ people face in every aspect of their lives: in housing, employment, health care, retirement, and basic human rights.

INDEX

PICTURE CREDITS

Cover: Canan Turan/iStockphoto.com

4: Osugi/Shutterstock.com (top left)

4: Oldrich/Shutterstock.com (top right)4: Olga Popova/Shutter-stock.com (bottom left)

4: lazyllama/Shutterstock.com (bottom right)

5: Lisa F. Young/Shutterstock.com (top)

5: Featureflash Photo Agency/Shutterstock.com (bottom)

8: CREATISTA/Shutterstock.com

12: Natan Dvir/Polaris/Newscom

15: Associated Press

19: Heather Shimmin/Shutterstock.com

24: Brian F Alpert/ZUMAPRESS/Newscom

28: Associated Press

32: Associated Press

36: NIBSC/Science Source

39: AP Images for AIDS Healthcare Foundation

44: Frances Roberts/agefotostock/Newscom

47: WendyOlsenPhotography/iStock.com

53: Associated Press

56: Featureflash Photo Agency/Shutterstock.com

60: Jonathan Alcorn/ZUMAPRESS/Newscom

64: Associated Press

69: ABA/Newscom